SHAPE IT! 4

COMBO A

STUDENT'S BOOK

WITH DIGITAL PACK

Samantha Lewis
with Daniel Vincent

CAMBRIDGE
UNIVERSITY PRESS

CONTENTS

STARTER

WELCOME!

VOCABULARY

Travel

S.01 **1 Match the words in the box with the photos. Then listen, check, and repeat.**

accommodation	☐	sightseeing	1
backpacking	☐	tourist attractions	☐
resort	☐	trip	☐

1 
2 
3 
4 
5 
6 

S.02 **2 Complete the comments with the words from Exercise 1. Then, listen and check.**

Where did you go on vacation this summer?

London. It's a great city for [1] ______________ because there are so many [2] ______________, like Big Ben.

To a [3] ______________ in Greece. The [4] ______________ was amazing – a beautiful hotel right next to the beach.

I went [5] ______________ in Mexico this summer – just me, my bag, and a paper map. It was the best [6] ______________ of my life.

LEARN TO LEARN

Personalizing Vocabulary

Writing sentences helps you remember words.

Use It!

3 Write true sentences about your vacations with the words in Exercise 1.

____

____

____

Music and Theater

S.03 **4 Match the nouns in the box with the definitions. Then listen, check, and repeat.**

audience lines part rehearsal scene show

1 when people practice a play ______________
2 live performance in a theater ______________
3 the words actors say ______________
4 a character in a play ______________
5 the people who watch ______________
6 a part of a play ______________

Use It!

5 Complete the questions with words from Exercise 4. Discuss the questions.

1 Have you ever been in a ______________ at school? What ______________ did you play? How did you learn your ______________? Did you have any ______________ before the show?
2 How is the ______________ at the theater and movies different from at a concert?
3 If you were in a movie, would you want to appear all the way through the movie or be in one big, important ______________?

Explore It!

Guess the correct answer.

What movies do these lines come from?

a "To infinity and beyond!"
b "Just keep swimming."

Write other famous lines from movies in English. Can your partner guess the movie?

READING

An Interview in a School Magazine

S.04 **1** Look at the photo. What do you think the boy is doing? Read the interview and check your answer.

Now that we're back in school, everybody's talking about what they did during the summer. Some of you probably went to a resort or went sightseeing with your family, and most of you probably spent time at the pool with friends. But not Joshua Wills. His summer was very different. Let's find out why.

Joshua, you didn't have a normal summer vacation this year, did you? What did you do?

No, I didn't. I went to a theater camp for teenagers. Our teachers were real actors from the theater and TV. They taught us all about acting – you know, how to develop a character, how to project your voice and use your body. It was a lot of fun.

Did you put on a show?

We put on a musical about a detective. I played the part of the detective's assistant. We had one rehearsal every day for a week and then three performances. A lot of my friends and family came.

How did it go?

It was great, but on the first night, in the final scene, I forgot my lines. Everything was going really well and then suddenly I couldn't remember anything! Everyone in the audience was looking at me, thinking, "What's wrong? He's not speaking. He's not even moving!"

Were you panicking?

I wasn't panicking. I was just frozen! But in the end, I remembered the lines and it was all OK.

Do you want to do more theater?

Definitely! I don't want to stop. In fact, I'm writing a play. It's more difficult than I expected, but I'm really enjoying it. I want to put it on at school.

Are you looking for any actors?

Of course! Why? Do you want to join us?

Maybe! It sounds like fun!

2 Read the interview again and answer the questions.

1. Why was Joshua's summer vacation unusual? ____________
2. What did the theater camp participants learn? ____________
3. How often did the group practice their play? ____________
4. What problem did Joshua have? ____________
5. How did the audience react to the problem? ____________
6. Why is Joshua looking for actors now? ____________

3 Find words in the interview that mean …

1. speak loudly and clearly (phrase). ____________
2. somebody who helps someone do their job (n). ____________
3. unable to move (adj). ____________
4. 100 percent yes! (adv). ____________

Voice It!

4 Discuss the questions.

1. Joshua's teachers were real actors. What is good about this?
2. Have you ever acted or spoken in front of a big group of people? How was it?

GRAMMAR IN ACTION

Past and Present, Simple and Continuous

Watch video S.1
What did he do every day?
What's he doing now?

	Simple Present	Present Continuous	Simple Past	Past Continuous
+	It **sounds** like fun.	I [3] ____ **writing** a play.	We **had** one rehearsal every day.	Everyone in the audience [7] ____ **looking** at me.
–	I [1] ___don't___ **want** to stop.	He **isn't speaking**.	You [5] ____ **have** a normal summer vacation this year.	I [8] ____ **panicking**.
?	[2] ____ you **want** to join us?	[4] ____ you **looking** for any actors?	What [6] ____ you **do**?	**Were** you **panicking**?

1 **Complete the examples in the chart above with the correct form of *to be* or *to do*. Use the interview on page 5 to help you.**

S.05 **2** **Complete the sentences with the correct form of the verbs in parentheses. Then listen and check.**

1. Mike ___goes___ (go) sightseeing every year.
2. Amalia ________ (not learn) her lines until the night before the first show.
3. A Where's Harry? B He ________ (read) in his room.
4. You didn't like the play, did you, Eddie? You ________ (sleep) during it!
5. I'm so happy we ________ (not stay) in that resort last week when the terrible storm came.
6. Ana's not at the rehearsal because she ________ (not feel) well right now.

3 **Complete Esme's blog with the correct form of the verbs in the box.**

begin	do	get up	go	~~have~~	not finish	not forget	practice	start	think

Hi, everyone. Yesterday we [1] ___had___ our last rehearsal for the musical. I [2] ________ practicing until 11 p.m., and when I [3] ________ to bed, some of the others [4] ________ still ________. The first show [5] ________ at 7:30 tonight. I didn't feel nervous when I [6] ________ this morning, but I [7] ________ to feel nervous now – I hope I [8] ________ my lines. But I'm also really excited. I [9] ________ it's going to be a great night. Anyway, [10] ________ you ________ anything this weekend? Why don't you come and see me?

Use It!

4 **Write the questions.**

1. what / you / do / at nine o'clock last night
   What were you doing at nine o'clock last night?
2. what time / you / get up / today
   ____
3. during the summer / you / prefer to go sightseeing or go to the beach
   ____
4. what time / you / usually / get up / when you're on vacation
   ____
5. speak English to anyone / last week
   ____
6. what / you / wear / at the moment
   ____

5 **Ask and answer the questions.**

What were you doing at nine o'clock last night?

I was watching some videos online.

VOCABULARY AND LISTENING

Ways of Communicating

S.06 **1 Match the verbs in the box with emoticons 1–9. Then listen, check, and repeat.**

describe	☐	shake hands	1	translate	☐
greet	☐	shout	☐	wave	☐
post	☐	smile	☐	whisper	☐

S.07 **2 Listen to the conversations and circle the correct words from Exercise 1.**

1 whisper / shake hands
2 translate / smile
3 post / shout
4 greet / translate
5 wave / describe

3 Do we express the verbs in Exercise 1 with actions or words? Complete the chart.

Actions	Words
shake hands	*describe*

LEARN TO LEARN

Describing Words You Don't Know with Other Words or a Gesture

When you don't know a word, use words you do know to describe it or use gestures to express what you mean.

4 Express or explain the words in the box with other words or gestures.

accommodation cry dance frozen movie sing stand up tourist attraction

It's a place where you can stay. *Accommodation?*

Use It!

5 Use gestures or tell your partner *I do this when ....* Can they guess the verb?

A Talk

S.08 **6 Listen to Mateo and mark (✓) the tips that helped him learn English.**

a Describe a word with other words. ☐
b Take a language course. ☐
c Don't worry about making mistakes. ☐
d Listen to music. ☐
e Talk as much as possible. ☐
f Translate words and make them sound English. ☐
g Watch TV. ☐

S.08 **7 Listen again and complete each sentence with one word.**

1 Mateo is studying ________ in college.
2 He didn't understand the family at first because they ________ so fast.
3 When he doesn't know a word, he describes it or ________ it and makes a word in English similar to the Spanish word.
4 A lot of things were different for him, but he liked the ________ best.

Voice It!

8 Discuss the questions.

1 Which of Mateo's tips do you use?
2 Which tips would you like to try?

GRAMMAR IN ACTION

Present Perfect and Simple Past

Watch video S.2
Where did she go last summer?
Which language has she never studied?

	Present Perfect	Simple Past
+	I**'ve been** in college now for three months.	I **started** my course in October.
–	I **haven't stopped** [1] since I was there! I**'ve** [2]_______ **been** to New York.	I **met** a lot of people in the first few weeks.
?	**Have** you [3]_______ **been** to New York?	**Did** you **go** to New York last year?

1 **Complete the examples in the chart above with *ever*, *since*, or *never*.**

Get It Right!

We don't use the simple present with **since**.

We've been here since Tuesday.

NOT ~~We are here since Tuesday.~~

2 **Look at sentences a–d. Circle the correct options to complete the rules.**

a Last year, I **spent** six months in New York.

b I **didn't understand** the kids because they **spoke** fast.

c I**'ve met** so many interesting people!

d I**'ve stayed** in contact with people I **met** in New York.

1 Use the *present perfect* / *simple past* for things that happened in a finished time period, e.g., last year.

2 Use the *present perfect* / *simple past* for things that happened in the past in an unfinished time period or when the exact time of the action is not important.

3 S.09 **Circle the correct words. Then listen and check.**

BEN [1]*Have you ever been* / *Did you ever go* to a music festival?

JESSIE Yeah, [2]*I've been* / *went* to one this summer. It was great.

BEN Where [3]*has it been* / *was it*?

JESSIE Near the town where we [4]*have been* / *went* on vacation. [5]*We've stayed* / *stayed* in the town a lot of times, but this was our first time at the festival.

BEN What [6]*have you liked* / *did you like* best?

JESSIE The Night Owls [7]*have had* / *had* some amazing dancers and [8]*have sounded* / *sounded* incredible.

BEN [9]*I've never heard* / *didn't hear* of them.

JESSIE Oh, they're great! [10]*I've liked* / *liked* them for ages.

4 **Complete the text with the simple past or present perfect.**

I [1] have never been (be) to Mexico, but last summer I [2]__________ (get) a job in a Mexican restaurant. I [3]__________ (meet) tons of people since I [4]__________ (start) working there and I [5]__________ (make) friends. At first they [6]__________ (speak) to me in Spanish, but I [7]__________ (not understand). Since then I [8]__________ (go) to Spanish classes and I [9]__________ (learn) a lot. Our teacher [10]__________ (teach) us how to describe things when we don't know the exact word.

Use It!

5 **Discuss the questions.**

1 How many cities in your country have you visited?
2 How long have you known your best friend?
3 Have you ever been to a festival?

I've been to three cities. I went to the capital last month, but there are some cities I've never been to.

WRITING

An Informal Email

1 Look at the photos. What can you see? Read Azra's email and put the photos in the correct order.

a  ☐

b  ☐

c  ☐

2 Read the email again. Why did Azra write the email? What did she enjoy about her visit?

[1]From:	azra.kara@myemail.com
[2]To:	gaby.bates@myemail.com
[3]Subject:	Thank you

[4]Hi Gaby,

[5]How are things? [6]I just wanted to say thank you for a great visit to Seattle. I had an amazing time and your family is so kind!

I loved meeting your friends and visiting the city. There's so much to see! I learned so much about the U.S.A. that I didn't know before. I've listened to the playlist you made me a lot of times since I got back home, and I know all the words to the songs!

I've told my friends all about my trip and they're really looking forward to meeting you next month. I can't wait to take you sightseeing in Istanbul to show you all the tourist attractions and introduce you to my friends and family. We've bought tickets to go and watch a Turkish dance show while you're here – I hope you like it!

[7]Write back soon.

[8]Love, Azra

3 Match a–h with the parts of the email 1–8.

a address of the recipient ☐

b address of the sender 1

c ending and your name ☐

d first sentence ☐

e last sentence ☐

f reason you are writing ☐

g beginning and name ☐

h topic of the email ☐

4 Complete the *Useful Language* box with phrases from the email.

Useful Language

Starting and ending an informal email

Start + name: Hello Gaby, / [1] ____________,

First sentence: How are you? / Thanks for your email. / [2] ____________?

The reason you are writing: I'm writing to / [3] ____________

Last sentence: See you soon. / Bye for now. / [4] ____________.

End + name: Take care, Azra / [5] ____________

PLAN

5 Imagine you are writing an email to a penpal in an English-speaking country. You have visited their country. They are going to be visiting yours soon. Take notes.

Where did you go? ____________

____

What did you do? ____________

____

What did you like about your visit? ____________

____

What are you going to do when they visit you?

____

____

WRITE

6 Write your email. Remember to include language and vocabulary from this unit, phrases from the *Useful Language* box, the parts of the email in Exercise 3, and the ideas in Exercise 5.

CHECK

7 Do you …

- start and end the email correctly?
- give the reason why you are writing?
- say what you are going to do when your penpal visits?

1 What is fashion?

LEARNING OUTCOMES

I can ...

- understand texts about technology and fashion
- give my opinion politely
- comment on a blog entry
- understand how to use the present perfect simple and continuous and modifiers
- talk about and describe clothes and shoes
- categorize adjectives, record new verbs, compare British English and American English, and write different kinds of example sentences

Start It!

1 Look at the photo. Do you like the clothes that the people are wearing? Why / Why not?
2 Before you watch, what does fashion mean to you?
3 Name three ways fashion changed in the 1960s. Watch and check.
4 What is your favorite fashion style?

Watch video 1.1

p13

Grammar in Action 1.2

p15

Grammar in Action 1.3

p16

Everyday English 1.4

p18

Globetrotters 1.5

VOCABULARY
Describing Clothes and Shoes

1.01 **1** **Match the adjectives in bold with the numbers in the photos. Then listen, check, and repeat.**

baggy jeans	☐	**long-sleeved** dress	☐
checkered skirt	☐	**plain cotton** T-shirt	☐
denim skirt	☐	**polka-dot** shoes	☐
flowery dress	☐	**striped** T-shirt	☐
high-heeled boots	☐	**tight** jeans	1
leather shoes	☐		

1.02 **2** **Alex and Isabel are shopping for clothes for a school party. Listen to the conversation. Which things in Exercise 1 do they buy?**

____

____

LEARN TO LEARN

Categorizing

When we use a lot of adjectives to describe one thing, we use this order: shape, color, pattern, material.

3 **Complete the chart with the adjectives from Exercise 1.**

Shape	Pattern	Material
baggy		

4 **Write three sentences describing the clothes in Exercise 1. Use at least two adjectives in each sentence.**

1 *She's wearing a blue cotton T-shirt.*
2 ______________________________
3 ______________________________
4 ______________________________

5 **Read your sentences in Exercise 4. Can your partner guess which person you are describing?**

Use It!

6 **Discuss the questions.**

1 Which clothes in Exercise 1 do you have?
2 Can you describe the clothes you are wearing?
3 Which shapes, patterns, and materials do you usually wear? Which do you never wear?

Explore It!

Guess the correct answer.

Some celebrities wear special "anti-paparazzi" scarves. What do you think these scarves do?

a make their faces more beautiful
b make the photos turn black
c make the celebrities look ugly

Find out about a clothing designer. Write a question for your partner to answer.

Fashion & Technology

CONNECTED CLOTHES

Anyone who has been reading my blog for a while knows that I'm a huge fan of technology in fashion. Here are my latest discoveries.

1 ☐ We've all seen watches that measure how much we move or sleep, but what about a T-shirt? Over the last few years, scientists have been developing clothes that can record information about our heart rate or breathing and that can help us stay healthy. Most people have a denim jacket. But have you ever seen a denim jacket that can play music or send instant messages? Well, scientists have designed one that can. You just have to touch the sleeve and your music starts playing!

2 ☐ Scientists have also created clothes with sensors that take our body temperature and circulate warm or cool air through the material so that we never feel too hot or too cold. Special clothes for astronauts or emergency service workers have been using this technology for years, but now companies have created similar materials for everyday clothing and shoes. Great! No more hot, sweaty feet!

3 ☐ Now there are even smart clothes that produce energy while we're wearing them! Scientists in South Korea have created a material that turns movement into electricity. So you can charge your phone while you're doing exercise or just walking around! That's smart!

4 ☐ Finally, if you haven't been following my updates on 3-D printing, check out these trendy designs. My favorite is the high-heeled shoes. I love the fact that each design is individual and that one day we'll be able to design and print our own patterned or plain clothes and shoes at home.

READING

A Blog Entry

1 **Look at the pictures. How do they combine technology and fashion?**

1.03 2 **Read the blog entry. Match headings a–d with paragraphs 1–4.**

- a 3-D Printed Clothes
- b Clothes That Change Temperature
- c Connected Clothing
- d Energy-Producing Clothes

3 **Read the blog entry again and answer the questions.**

1. How can we watch our health with connected clothing?
 ______
2. How does the denim jacket in the text play music?
 ______
3. What's good about creating electricity with clothes?
 ______
4. What does the blogger predict about 3-D printed clothes?
 ______

4 **Find words in the blog that mean …**

1. the part of clothing that covers your arm (1). ______
2. to move around something (2). ______
3. to put electricity into a device like a phone (3). ______
4. the latest information (4). ______
5. to produce something with a printer (4). ______

Voice It!

5 **Discuss the questions.**

1. Would you like to have any of the smart clothes in the blog?
2. What other things would you like clothes to do in the future?
3. Do you think smart clothes are important? Why / Why not?

Finished? p118 Ex. 1

Watch video 1.2
How long has Tara been knitting?
How many people have bought Patrick's shoes?

GRAMMAR IN ACTION

Present Perfect Simple and Present Perfect Continuous

	Present Perfect Simple	Present Perfect Continuous
+	Scientists [1] have also **created** clothes with sensors.	Over the last few years, scientists [3] ______ **been developing** clothes that can record information.
–	He **hasn't bought** any 3-D printed clothing yet.	If you [4] ______ **been following** my updates on 3-D printing, check out these trendy designs.
?	[2] ______ you ever **seen** a denim jacket that can play music?	How long **have** you **been reading** my blog?

1 **Complete the examples in the chart above with the correct form of *to have*.**

2 **Complete the rules with *simple* or *continuous*.**

1. In present perfect ______ sentences, the focus is on the result of an activity.
2. In present perfect ______ sentences, the focus is on how long the activity is.

3 **Put the words in the correct order to make sentences.**

1. a lot of / I've / blog entries / written / .
   I've written a lot of blog entries.
2. since / a fashion blog / writing / She's been / January / .
   ______
3. made / Have you / your own clothes / ever / ?
   ______
4. been / He's / two years / designing / for / clothes / .
   ______

1.04 **4** **Complete the text with the present perfect continuous form of the verbs in the box. Then listen and check.**

help	make	not practice	~~try~~	watch	work

Recently I [1] 've been trying to learn how to knit. It's really difficult! I [2] ______ a lot of videos online, but I [3] ______ very much. I [4] ______ a scarf for a few days now, but it's full of holes and looks awful. My mom [5] ______ me, too, but she [6] ______ all week and doesn't really have much free time.

1.05 **5** **Complete the sentences with the present perfect simple or continuous form of the verbs in parentheses. Then listen, check, and repeat.**

1. How long has he been designing clothes? (design)
2. ______ you ever ______ to knit? (learn)
3. She ______ never ______ high-heeled shoes. (wear)
4. I ______ in these shoes all morning and my feet really hurt! (walk)

Use It!

6 **Imagine you are a fashion designer. Make questions with the present perfect simple or continuous. Then think of your answers.**

1. What / designed?
   ______
2. Who / worn your designs?
   ______
3. How long / designing clothes?
   ______

7 **Ask and answer the questions. Which designer makes the most interesting clothes? Why?**

I've designed a coat that changes color when it gets wet!

Finished? p118 Ex. 2

VOCABULARY AND LISTENING

Verbs Related to Clothes and Shoes

1.06 **1** **Read the fashion forum and match the verbs in bold with the definitions. Then listen, check, and repeat.**

ARE YOU A FOLLOWER OF FASHION?

MARIA I don't buy many clothes because they **go out of style** so quickly. I usually buy things that **go with** other clothes I already have. I like wearing green clothes because they **match** my eyes!

GISELA I'm really tall, so it's difficult to find clothes that **fit** me, especially jeans! I wear jeans so much they **wear out**! A lot of clothes don't **look good on** me because they haven't been designed for tall people.

EDU I love fashion and I work in a clothing store on Saturdays. It's great because I get to try on tons of clothes. The worst part is the dressing rooms. People leave clothes on the floor and I have to **hang up** the jackets and pants and **fold** all the T-shirts. It takes forever!

IRINA Today I had a complete fashion disaster. I was trying on a dress in a store. I managed to **zip** it **up**! But when I tried to take the dress off, I couldn't **unzip** it. How embarrassing!

1. be the right size _fit_
2. not popular any longer ________
3. wear something so much it looks old ________
4. make someone look nice ________
5. look good together ________
6. be similar or the same color/type ________
7. close zippers ________
8. open zippers ________
9. put clothes on a hanger ________
10. bend clothes so that one part lies on another part ________

Get It Right!

The word **clothes** is always plural.

Your new clothes look great!

LEARN TO LEARN

Recording New Verbs

Make sentences with new verbs so that you can remember how to use them.

2 **Complete the sentences with the correct form of the verbs in the box and the words in parentheses.**

hang up	look good on	not go with	~~wear out~~	zip up

1. You never _wear out your shoes_. They always look new. (your shoes)
2. That color ________. It matches your eyes. (you)
3. This top ________. They're different styles. (my skirt)
4. ________. It's cold. (your jacket)

3 EXAM **Discuss the questions.**

Student A:
What kinds of clothes do you like to wear?
Which clothes fit you well?

Student B:
What kinds of clothes don't you like to wear?
Which clothes look good on you?

An Interview

1.07 **4** **Listen to an interview with Carla. Where does she get her clothes from?**

1.07 **5** **Listen again and complete the text.**

Carla started looking at fashion designs online when she was [1] _12_. She enjoys upcycling – creating [2] ________ from something that exists. She also decorates [3] ________ T-shirts and tops with her own designs. She knows that people buy fast fashion because the clothes are [4] ________ and that ethical fashion is [5] ________ than fast fashion, but ethical fashion thinks about the people who [6] ________.

Pronunciation p141

GRAMMAR IN ACTION
Modifiers

Watch video 1.3
What are the top three fashion mistakes?
What's the problem if your bedroom is totally messy?

I've been [1] totally obsessed with fashion since I was a child.	**a** extremely / absolutely / totally / really
They look [2] ________ good.	**b** fairly / ________
These clothes are [3] ________ more expensive …	**c** ________ / a little
but they last [4] ________ longer.	**d** ________ / far

1 **Complete the examples in the chart above with *a bit*, *a lot*, *pretty*, and *totally*. Use the same words in each row.**

2 **Which words (a–d) do we use before …**

1 comparative adjectives to show a big difference? ________
2 comparative adjectives to show a small difference? ________
3 adjectives to intensify them? ________
4 adjectives to mean more than *a little* but less than *very*? ________

1.10 **3** **Circle the correct words. Then listen and check.**

Making materials like cotton or denim can be [1]*extremely / a lot* damaging to the environment. That's why it's [2]*absolutely / far* essential to create new materials from natural products that are [3]*fairly / a lot* better for the planet. Some materials, like bamboo, have been [4]*fairly / a little* successful. Others are still being developed, like a material from the rice plant, which is [5]*really / a bit* similar to cotton, and one made from chicken feathers, which is [6]*pretty / a bit* warm, like wool. Technology has also made it [7]*really / far* easier to recycle materials like plastic bottles into clothes such as leggings and T-shirts, which is [8]*really / a lot* good news for the environment!

4 **Complete the sentences with the words in parentheses.**

1 I feel pretty tired today. I need to sleep well, or I'll be extremely tired tomorrow. (extremely / pretty)
2 The shopping mall in our town is ________ good, but the one outside town is ________ better. (fairly / far)
3 He creates ________ amazing designs, which are ________ more fun than ours. (a lot / totally)
4 I'm ________ good at art, but there are people in my class who are ________ more talented than me. (far / fairly)
5 This coat is ________ beautiful and it's only ________ more expensive than the other one. (absolutely / a bit)

Use It!

5 **Complete the sentences so they are true for you.**

1 I am pretty good at ________________.
2 I feel really sad when ________________.
3 A subject I find a lot easier than before is ________________.
4 I'm a bit more interested in ________________ than before.
5 I think it's absolutely amazing that ________________.

6 **Guess what your partner wrote in their sentences. Score one point for each correct guess.**

Did you say, "I am pretty good at English?"

No, I didn't. I said, "I'm pretty good at art."

Finished? p118 Ex. 3

SPEAKING

Giving Your Opinion Politely

1.11 **1 Listen to the conversation. Does Diego like the things?**

DIEGO Hey, Dana. How's it going?
DANA Hi, Diego. I've been shopping all morning. I've bought some great stuff. Do you want to see?
DIEGO Yeah, sure.
DANA I got this striped jacket from Zaps, that new store they've just opened.
DIEGO Oh, right. Wow! [1]That's … uh … different!
DANA I know! It's totally out there!
DIEGO Hmm, [2]_______________ yellow and blue together, but the blue matches the color of your eyes.
DANA Thanks! And check out these pants.
DIEGO Flowery pants! Wow! Very retro!
DANA I know! They fit really well. What do you think?
DIEGO Well, [3]_______________, but I can see why you like them.
DANA Do you think they look good on me?
DIEGO Yes, I guess so.
DANA I think I might wear them to go out later, with the jacket.
DIEGO Hmm, [4]_______________ I'd wear them together. [5]_______________ the pants would go better with a plain top.
DANA No, patterns are totally in this year.
DIEGO You're such a fashion victim, Dana!

1.11 **2 Complete the conversation with the phrases from the *Useful Language* box. Then listen again and check.**

Useful Language

I don't know if …
I'm not a huge fan of …
I think maybe …
That's … uh … different!
they're not exactly my style

3 Match the meanings (1–4) with the words and phrases in the *Everyday English* box.

1 someone who follows fashion
2 fashionable
3 different
4 look at

Watch video 1.4
Everyday English

check out ☐ fashion victim ☐
in ☐ out there ☐

PLAN

4 In your notebook, write about the clothes on the right.

What clothes are they?
Who bought them and why?
What do they look like?
Why do you like or not like them?

SPEAK

5 Practice the conversation with your partner. Remember to use the present perfect simple and continuous, modifiers, vocabulary from this unit, and phrases from the *Useful Language* and *Everyday English* boxes.

CHECK

6 Work with another pair. Listen to their conversation and complete the notes.

Who bought them and why? _______________
____

What do they look like? _______________
____

Does the other pair like them? Why / Why not?
____

Four Steps

to Reduce Your Fashion Footprint

Here are some ideas you can try!

- Have a clothing swap party. Swap clothes you don't want with your friends.
- Save energy. Wash clothes less often, dry clothes naturally, don't iron!
- Give old clothes to secondhand stores. Don't throw them away!
- Buy fewer, better quality new clothes.

Comments

Great post! It got me thinking about how to reduce my fashion footprint. I talked to my parents and we decided to try reduce the amount of energy we use on our clothes. Usually we wash all our clothes every time we wear them, even when they're still pretty clean; but this month we've been washing clothes less often, and we haven't ironed anything. My parents have saved money and I've been much better at hanging up my clothes! **Carlos**

Thanks for sharing! I had no idea that I throw so many clothes away! I had a clothing swap party last week. I got a great denim jacket that I absolutely love! I also got two long-sleeved tops and some cool high-heeled boots for free! I was absolutely amazed that we swapped everything! Since reading your post, I've decided to buy far fewer new clothes in the future. **Amie**

WRITING

A Blog Comment

1 **Look at the blog entry. How can people reduce their fashion footprint?**

2 **Read the blog comments. Answer the questions.**

1. Were the ideas that Carlos and Amie tried successful? How do you know?
   ______
2. What does Amie want to do in the future?
   ______

3 **Find the phrases from the *Useful Language* box in the blog comments. Which phrases can you use when you …**

1. enjoy reading a post?
   ______
2. learn something new from the post?
   ______
3. change your behavior because of the post?
   ______

Useful Language

Great post! I had no idea that …
It got me thinking about … Since reading your post, I've …
Thanks for sharing! We decided to …

PLAN

4 **Write your own blog comment. Look at the ideas in the blog entry and take notes about which one to write about.**

Which idea will you try out? ______

Do you think it will go well? Why / Why not?
______

What other ideas would you like to try in the future? ______

WRITE

5 **Write your blog comment. Remember to include the present perfect simple and continuous, modifiers, vocabulary from this unit, and phrases from the *Useful Language* box.**

CHECK

6 **Do you …**

- explain why an idea might or might not work well?
- explain what you would like to try in the future?

Finished? p118 Ex. 4

AROUND THE WORLD

READING
A Travel Guide

Globetrotters
Watch video 1.5
What We Wear and Why

- Why do we wear clothes and what do they show about us?
- What is a *deel* and why do Mongolian people wear it?
- What do the colors blue, white, green, yellow, and orange represent for the Masai people?

1.12 **1 Are the sentences *T* (true) or *F* (false)? Read the travel guide and check your answers.**

1 Kilts have not always been made of tartan. ___
2 Tartans today indicate where people live. ___
3 Scottish dress is different for men and women. ___
4 Tartan patterns are popular outside Scotland. ___

Voice It!

2 Discuss the questions.

1 Why do you think Scottish people wear traditional clothing for special occasions?
2 What traditional clothing do people wear in your country?
3 Why is it important to celebrate cultural traditions?

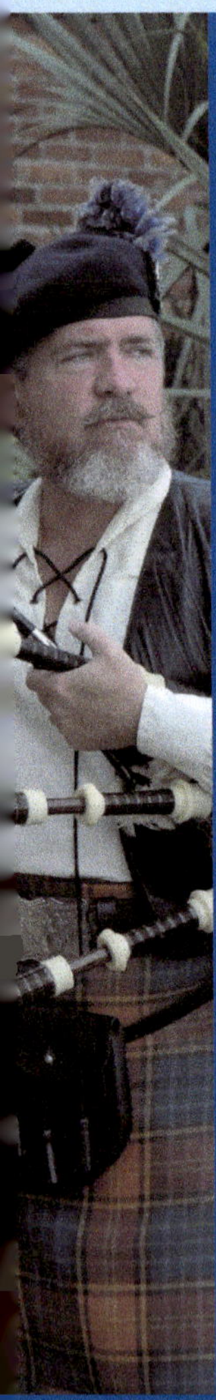

Traditional Scottish Dress

You have probably seen photos of Scotland's most famous piece of clothing, the kilt. But did you know that Scottish men have been wearing kilts for centuries? A kilt used to be an extremely long piece of heavy plain material that men from the Scottish Highlands wore every day. They wrapped the material around their waist and over one shoulder to protect them from the cold wind or rain. Nowadays, the design of the kilt is totally different. It is a knee-length **woolen** skirt, with a pattern of vertical and horizontal stripes in different colours called **tartan**. Tartan designs used to indicate the area where people lived and were far less colourful than they are today. Since the 18th century, people have been wearing designs that represent their family name or clan (group of families), and today there are over 4,500 designs! The kilt forms part of the traditional Highland **dress**, which is quite different for men and women (see box).

Highland dress is extremely popular in Scotland for special occasions such as weddings, funerals, or parties, particularly for men. Women often wear kilts to do traditional Scottish dancing at sports and cultural events. Nowadays, tartan isn't just used for traditional dress in Scotland. Fashion designers around the world use tartan to create modern designs such as tartan **trousers** or tartan shoes, and celebrities from Rihanna to Shawn Mendes have been photographed wearing tartan. Even though people have worn tartan for centuries, it is still popular today.

MEN:
- tartan kilt and a kilt pin
- leather belt
- sporran (a small leather or fur bag that hangs from the belt.)
- plain or tartan socks
- kilt knife (a small knife kept in one sock)
- ghillies (plain, flat leather shoes)

WOMEN:
- long or knee-length tartan kilt
- tartan shawl (a piece of material worn over your shoulders)
- plain or tartan socks
- ghillies

3 **Use the travel guide to complete the chart.**

Kilts in the 18th Century	Highland Dress for Men	Who wears traditional tartan clothes?
One long piece of cloth worn around waist and over shoulder		
Kilts in the 21st Century	**Highland Dress for Women**	**Who wears modern tartan clothes?**

LEARN TO LEARN

British English vs. American English

4 **Read the definitions and write the British English word from the text.**

1 The American English word for a pattern of vertical and horizontal stripes is *plaid*. ________________
2 A word for a set of clothes. In American English, we say *attire*. ________________
3 This clothing item covers your legs. In American English, we say *pants*. ________________
4 The American English adjective for this material is *wool*. ________________

5 **Write the American English spellings for these words.**

1 colourful ________________
2 favourite ________________
3 organise ________________
4 flavour ________________
5 centre ________________
6 neighbour ________________
7 traveller ________________
8 programme ________________

6 **Think and discuss with a partner. What other words or structures are different in British English?**

Explore It!

Guess the correct answer.

It was illegal to wear tartan in the middle of the 18th century in Scotland. True or false?

Find another fact about traditional dress. Write a question for your partner to answer.

SHAPE IT!

CULTURE PROJECT

A Fact File

A fact file presents key information about a topic. Make a fact file about traditional clothing from your culture.

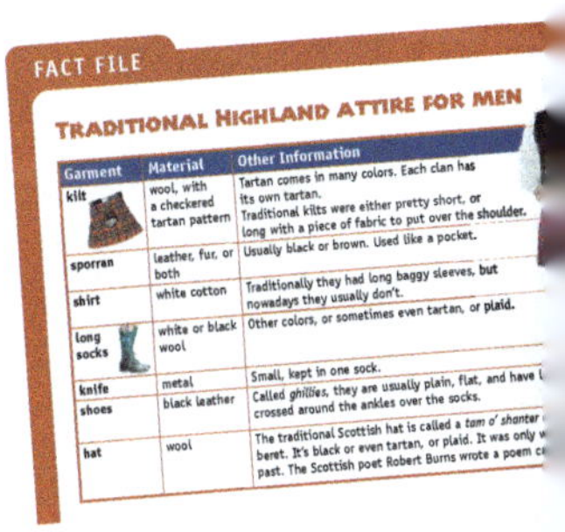

FACT FILE

TRADITIONAL HIGHLAND ATTIRE FOR MEN

Garment	Material	Other Information
kilt	wool, with a checkered tartan pattern	Tartan comes in many colors. Each clan has its own tartan. Traditional kilts were either pretty short, or long with a piece of fabric to put over the shoulder.
sporran	leather, fur, or both	Usually black or brown. Used like a pocket.
shirt	white cotton	Traditionally they had long baggy sleeves, but nowadays they usually don't.
long socks	white or black wool	Other colors, or sometimes even tartan, or plaid.
knife	metal	Small, kept in one sock.
shoes	black leather	Called *ghillies*, they are usually plain, flat, and have l crossed around the ankles over the socks.
hat	wool	The traditional Scottish hat is called a *tam o' shanter* beret. It's black or even tartan, or plaid. It was only w past. The Scottish poet Robert Burns wrote a poem c

Teacher's Resource Bank

1 REVIEW

VOCABULARY

1 Circle the word that doesn't fit.

1	baggy	tight	polka-dot
2	cotton	long-sleeved	denim
3	flowery	leather	plain
4	cotton	striped	checkered
5	plain	long-sleeved	high-heeled

2 Match 1–5 with a–e.

1 **Hang up** your clothes. ☐
2 I can't **unzip** my jacket. ☐
3 These jeans are **worn out** ☐
4 This T-shirt **doesn't fit** me anymore ☐
5 Your glasses really **look good on** you. ☐

a because I've had them for ages.
b because it's too small.
c The zipper's broken.
d You look great!
e They're all over the floor.

GRAMMAR IN ACTION

3 Complete the text with the present perfect simple or continuous form of the verbs in parentheses.

Sixteen-year-old Moziah Bridges [1]____________ (design) ties since he was nine. His grandmother taught him to make bow ties and since then he [2]____________ (own) his own business. The designer [3]____________ (appear) in magazines and on TV and [4]____________ (make) a collection of ties for basketball teams in the U.S.A. Mo is still in school but [5]____________ (work) in the evenings. It [6]____________ (not be) easy, but his mom helps him and he [7]____________ (employ) more people as his business [8]____________ (grow). Mo often gives talks to other people who [9]____________ (think) about starting a business.

4 Circle the correct modifier to complete the sentences.

1 It takes *a little* / *extremely* longer to fold your clothes, but then you don't have to iron them.
2 Where did you get that jacket? I *far* / *absolutely* love it!
3 The second movie in the series was *a bit* / *pretty* better than the first one, but not much.
4 I'm *a lot* / *fairly* good at speaking Chinese, but I can't write it.
5 I'm *far* / *totally* confused by his explanation. I don't understand it at all.
6 Have you seen this video? It's *really* / *a lot* funny.
7 That T-shirt is *far* / *really* nicer than the other one, but it's *really* / *a lot* expensive.

Self-Assessment

I can describe clothes and shoes.	☹	😐	☺
I can talk about clothes and shoes.	☹	😐	☺
I can use the present perfect simple and present perfect continuous.	☹	😐	☺
I can use modifiers.	☹	😐	☺

LEARN TO ... WRITE DIFFERENT KINDS OF EXAMPLE SENTENCES

You can write different kinds of example sentences to help you understand and remember new words.

1 **Read Ela's blog. Why does she recommend using the different kinds of example sentences to remember new words?**

Ela's English Learning BLOG

Today's Tip: Example Sentences

Hi, everyone! Today we're looking at a great way to learn vocabulary: example sentences. When I learn new words, I often use them in sentences to help me learn and remember them. There are different types of example sentences you can use. They're all good for different reasons.

a Sentences about you, your family, or your friends – when you use words in sentences about things people you know have done, the words are easier to remember.

b Funny sentences – a funny image can help the word stay in your memory.

c Sentences that explain the word – these make the meaning clear, like the examples in dictionaries.

Here are some of my latest examples. Can you guess which types they are?

1 I prefer **plain** T-shirts to ones with writing or pictures on them.

2 Your skin gets **sweaty** when you're hot or exercise a lot.

3 My baby brother always wipes his nose on his **sleeve**.

4 The giraffe couldn't **zip up** his jacket because it was too long!

5 A **checkered** pattern is a pattern of squares of different colors.

6 I thought I saw a zebra – but it was a horse in a black and white **striped** T-shirt.

So ... that's all from me today. Don't forget to share some example sentences of your own. You can post them below!

2 **Match Ela's examples 1–6 with types a–c.**

1 ______ 4 ______

2 ______ 5 ______

3 ______ 6 ______

SHAPE IT!

3 **Choose five words from the box and write an example sentence for each one. Use all of Ela's types (a–c) at least once.**

baggy	charge
fashion victim	fold
hang up	high-heeled
leather	not go with
polka-dot	updates

1 ______________________

2 ______________________

3 ______________________

4 ______________________

5 ______________________

4 **Tell your partner your sentences from Exercise 3. Which types (a–c) are they? Which sentences are your favorites and why?**

2 What can you change?

LEARNING OUTCOMES

I can …

- understand texts about international exchanges and a mystery object
- explain how to use something
- write an opinion essay
- understand how to use *used to* and *would* for past habits, the simple past, and the past perfect with *never, ever, already, by (then), by the time*
- talk about changes and parts of objects
- practice learning new words by using them in different situations, identify key words to understand audio texts, and help my classmates improve their writing
- make a history exhibition

Start It!

1 Look at the photo. Do you know what this animal is and how it changes?
2 Before you watch, how do you think cities change over time?
3 Which two events changed the city of Seoul? Watch and check.
4 How has your town or city changed?

Watch video 2.1

p25

Grammar in Action 2.2

p27

Grammar in Action 2.3

p28

Everyday English 2.4

VOCABULARY
Phrasal Verbs: Changes

1 **Which of the phrases a–l describes picture 1? Which phrase describes picture 2?**

a **settle down** in a new school
b **look forward to** the weekend
c **sign up** for French classes
d **try out** a new restaurant
e **turn out** well
f **move out** of a house
g **move to** a new school
h **go back** to the beginning
i **end up** in the wrong place
j **go through** a hard time
k **do without** the Internet
l **turn down** an invitation

1

2

2.01 2 **Match definitions 1–12 with phrasal verbs a–l from Exercise 1. Then listen, check, and repeat.**

1 feel happy about something in the future [b]
2 not have something [ ]
3 finally be in a place/situation [ ]
4 experience [ ]
5 stop living in a particular place [ ]
6 try something new [ ]
7 start to feel happy in a new place/situation [ ]
8 return [ ]
9 join an organized activity [ ]
10 say no to something [ ]
11 have a particular result [ ]
12 change to [ ]

2.02 3 **Listen to six conversations and complete the sentences using the correct form of the phrasal verbs from Exercise 1.**

1 He decides to ________________ for classes.
2 Molly ________________ the game.
Andre ________________ the invitation.
3 Tom ________________ a hard time now.
He ________________ in his new school.
4 Jo asks Ed to ________________ to the beginning.
5 They're going to ________________ the restaurant.
6 In the end, the party ________________ well.

LEARN TO LEARN
Using Words in Different Situations

Using new words in different situations helps you remember them.

4 **Think of different situations for the phrasal verbs in Exercise 1.**

What can you look forward to?

A party … the end of exams …

Use It!

5 **Think of questions using the phrasal verbs in Exercise 1. Ask and answer.**

Have you tried out a new restaurant recently?

Yes. We went to a great Italian restaurant last week.

Explore It!

Guess the correct answer.

How many students study in a foreign country every year?

a 2 million b 5 million c 11 million

Find out a fact about students in your country. Write a question for your partner.

A+ EXCHANGES – DISCOVER A NEW WORLD AND A NEW YOU!

Student Testimonials

LUCY

I love school here – it's so different from the U.S.A. Students have almost no homework and very few exams. At my school, we don't even have school subjects. We study topics and do projects instead. It's a great way to learn.

This experience has really helped me become more confident. I didn't use to be adventurous, but I've tried a lot of new things since I arrived here eight months ago. For example, I went on a reindeer safari on my birthday, and I've been going ice-swimming every Saturday. Plus, I've made a lot of friends. Finns are very cool people.

It hasn't all been easy. Winter is very hard because it's really dark – there are only three or four hours of light every day. The good thing is that you can see the beautiful Northern Lights.

If you get the opportunity to study abroad, don't turn it down, especially not if you can come to Finland!

BEN

Last year, I spent six wonderful months in Mexico. I used to dream about living in a different country, so when I discovered A+ Exchanges, I signed up immediately. It was an absolutely incredible experience. I loved the mix of local, European, and African cultures, and the people were really outgoing.

Of course, I went through some ups and downs at first, especially dealing with a different school system. For example, many Mexican schools have two schedules. Some students start school at 7:30 a.m., and some – like me – start at 2 p.m. We would finish at 8 p.m.! Also, I didn't speak much Spanish when I arrived, so it was really difficult to follow lessons. But my classmates would always help me, and I improved a lot.

I felt a bit homesick from time to time, but now I feel like I have two homes. In fact, I've decided to go to college there. I'm really looking forward to going back.

READING
A Brochure

1 **Look at the photos. Which show Finland? Which show Mexico? What do you think it is like to live there?**

2 **Read the brochure. Write *L* (Lucy) or *B* (Ben).** (2.03)

Which person …

1. has been abroad for more than half a year? ___
2. found the country's education system difficult? ___
3. has changed in a positive way? ___
4. found part of the year difficult because of the light? ___
5. likes the variety of cultures? ___
6. can do something better than they used to do? ___

3 **Find words in the brochure that mean …**

1. happy to try new things (Lucy). ________
2. from the nearby area (Ben). ________
3. friendly and sociable (Ben). ________
4. a mix of good and bad experiences (Ben). ________
5. missing your family (Ben). ________

4 **Read the sentences and write *T* (true), *F* (false), or *DS* (doesn't say).**

1. In Finland, students never take exams. ___
2. Students have long breaks in Finland. ___
3. Lucy has been ice-swimming more than once. ___
4. Ben never wanted to leave the U.S.A. ___
5. Mexican students don't all finish school at the same time. ___
6. Ben wants to go back home soon. ___

Voice It!

5 **Discuss the questions.**

1. Can you think of a country you would like to go on an exchange to?
2. Why would you like to visit that country?
3. What do you think would be difficult about living there?

Finished? p119 Ex. 1

GRAMMAR IN ACTION
Used To, *Would*, and Simple Past

Watch video 2.2
What did her grandmother use to write on?
What did she use to do outdoors?

	Used To / Would	Simple Past
+	I [1] used **to** dream about living in a different country. My classmates [2] ________ always help me.	I **went** on a reindeer safari.
–	I **didn't** [3] ________ **to** be adventurous.	I **didn't speak** much Spanish.
?	**Did** Lucy **use to** be adventurous?	**Did** Ben **learn** a lot of Spanish?

Pronunciation p141

1 Complete the examples in the chart above with one word in each blank. Use the brochure on page 24 to help you.

2 Complete the rules with *used to*/*would* or *the simple past*.

1. We use __________ to talk about situations that continued and actions that happened more than once in the past.
2. We use __________ to talk about things that happened only once.

3 Complete the text with *used to* and the verbs in parentheses.

My grandfather's childhood was different from mine. When he was a boy, he never [1] used to have (have) many toys, but he [2] __________ (have) a lot of time. He [3] __________ (love) playing outside. Sometimes, his friends [4] __________ (play) outside all day – they [5] __________ (go) out early and then they [6] __________ (come) home late at night. I think it [7] __________ (be) safer for children then.

Get It Right!

We use ***would*** with repeated past actions, not situations.

We would ride our bikes after school.

NOT ~~*We would live in Texas.*~~

4 Circle the correct words. Sometimes both are possible.

1. More people *would* / *used to* live in the country than in cities. Now it's the opposite.
2. In the past, TV channels *would* / *used to* stop at night.
3. Some people *didn't use to* / *wouldn't* smile in photos because their teeth were bad.
4. Many people *would* / *used to* think that the Earth was flat.

5 Complete the sentences with *used to*, *didn't use to*, or the simple past and the verbs in parentheses.

1. For his birthday, Aidan got (get) a new bike. He loved it.
2. Ada __________ (like) apples much, but now she does.
3. I __________ (end up) in the wrong place yesterday because I didn't have a map.
4. When Bill was younger, he __________ (turn down) invitations all the time because he was so shy.

Use It!

6 Write questions for a partner about their parents' lives with *used to* or the simple past.

1. what toys / play with ____________________
2. study English / at school ____________________
3. how / meet ____________________

7 Ask and answer the questions.

What toys did your parents use to play with?

I think they used to play with wooden toys, and they would often play outside.

Finished? p119 Ex. 2

VOCABULARY AND LISTENING

Parts of Objects

1 Look at the photos. Which objects do you recognize?

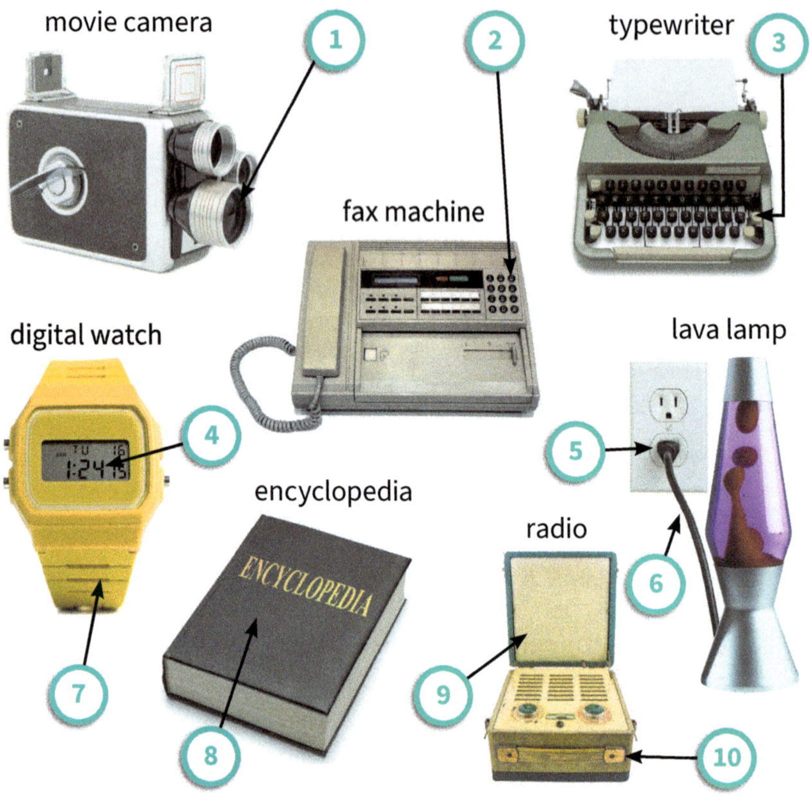

2.08 2 Match the words in the box with parts of the objects 1–10. Then listen, check, and repeat.

button ☐	cover ☐	handle ☐	lens 1	plug ☐
cord ☐	display ☐	key ☐	lid ☐	strap ☐

2.09 3 Circle the correct words. Then listen and check.

1 When you carry a backpack, do you use one *strap* / *cord* or both? Why?

2 Do you always put the *handle* / *lid* back on the peanut butter jar after using it?

3 How often do you clean the *key* / *lens* of the camera on your phone?

4 Without looking, can you remember what is on the *cover* / *display* of this book?

5 Can you name six objects that have an on/off *plug* / *button*?

6 Do you take your phone charger *cord* / *display* with you when you go out?

Use It!

4 Ask and answer the questions in Exercise 3. Are your answers similar or different?

A Game Show

2.10 5 Listen to a game show about retro objects. Which three objects in Exercise 1 are mentioned?

LEARN TO LEARN

Identifying Key Words

Identifying key words before you listen can help you understand what you hear.

6 Read the parts of the sentences and underline the key words.

1 Joey pushes the buzzer too early because he …

a can't wait to play.

b doesn't understand the rules.

2 Nicola guesses the first object correctly because she …

a has seen one before.

b has heard of it before.

3 People had fax machines …

a in their houses.

b in their workplaces.

4 People used lava lamps …

a instead of lightbulbs.

b because they were attractive.

2.10 7 Listen again and circle the correct options to complete the sentences in Exercise 6.

Voice It!

8 Discuss the questions.

1 Do you know any retro objects that have come back in style?

2 What do you think of them?

GRAMMAR IN ACTION

Past Perfect with *Never, Ever, Already, By (Then), By the Time*

Watch video 2.3
Where did she go last week?
When were 3-D printers first developed?

+	This was before anyone **had** [1] ___ever___ **heard** of printers. They**'d** [2] ________ **gone** out of style **by the time** you were born.
–	I**'d heard** of fax machines before, but I**'d** [3] ________ **seen** one. I **hadn't started** yet.
?	**Had** you **ever seen** a digital watch before then?

1 **Complete the examples in the chart above with *already*, *ever*, or *never*.**

2 **Circle the correct words to complete the rules.**

1 *Already*, *never*, and *ever* come *before* / *after* the main verb.

2 *By the time* means *before* / *after* something happened.

3 **Answer the questions. Use the past perfect and the words in parentheses.**

1 How did you know what would happen in the movie? (already / read / the book)

I knew because I had already read the book.

2 Why did you get lost? (never / be / there before)

____

3 Did you get a ticket for the concert? No, (by the time / I went online / they / sell out)

____

4 How was the party? (already / end / when we got there)

____

2.11 4 **Complete the text with the simple past or the past perfect form of the verbs in parentheses. Then listen and check.**

Last year I [1] went (go) on an exchange to Moscow. I [2] ________ (never / travel) alone before, so I [3] ________ (feel) nervous at first. Before I [4] ________ (go), I [5] ________ (already / learn) to read the Russian alphabet, although I [6] ________ (not practice) speaking Russian. By the time I [7] ________ (leave), I [8] ________ (improve) a lot. Everybody in Moscow [9] ________ (be) really kind and friendly, but it [10] ________ (not be) easy to deal with the cold weather. I [11] ________ (not pack) enough warm clothes, so I had to buy some after I [12] ________ (arrive). Anyway, I can't wait to go back. I [13] ________ (not expect) to enjoy it so much before I actually [14] ________ (get) there, but in the end I really [15] ________ (do)!

Use It!

5 **Ask and answer the questions about the topics below. Use the past perfect.**

1 hear of / connected clothing?

2 see / a photo of 3-D printed clothes?

3 hear of / ice-swimming?

4 see / a photo of the Northern Lights?

Before you started using this book, had you ever heard of connected clothing?

No, I'd never heard of it, but now I want to know more! / Yes, I had. I'd already read about it online.

Finished? p119 Ex. 3

SPEAKING
Explaining How to Use Something

2.12 **1 Listen to the conversation. Which of the things in the box does the typewriter have?**

cord   display   keys   plug   speaker

JORGE What's that? [1] Is it some kind of computer?
MERI No, it's my grandpa's old typewriter.
JORGE Where's the display?
MERI There isn't one, and there's no plug or cord.
JORGE That's so old-school! How did it work?
MERI The paper would move as you typed. [2] ______________________ press the keys hard, but not too fast, or they get stuck. Try it out!
JORGE [3] ______________________
MERI That's it. Just imagine – people used to type books on these things!
JORGE No way! I can't even find the letters I want.
MERI You need to sign up for typing classes! They're in the same place as an ordinary keyboard.
JORGE Oh, no! [4] ______________________ How do I go back? There's no "delete" key.
MERI [5] ______________________ start all over again.
JORGE No, thanks! Anyway, how come your grandpa had this?
MERI He used to need it for work, but after a while he ended up buying a computer.
JORGE I'm not surprised! I'm glad they'd invented computers by the time I started school! I'd hate to do my homework on this!

2.12 **2 Complete the conversation with the phrases from the *Useful Language* box. Then listen again and check.**

Useful Language

Is it some kind of …?   I've messed it up.
Like this, you mean?   What you do is, you …
You'll have to …

3 Complete the sentences with the phrases in the *Everyday English* box.

1 Barry's not here yet. ______________________ – he's always late.
2 A Do I press this button here?
  B ______________________
3 Your new jacket's so ______________________. My dad used to have one like that.
4 Oh, no! I've lost my homework! I'll have to do it ______________________.

Watch video 2.4
Everyday English

all over again
I'm not surprised
old-school   That's it.

PLAN

4 Choose an object on page 26. Take notes on how to use it in your notebook.

SPEAK

5 Practice the explanation with your partner. Remember to use past tenses, vocabulary from this unit, and phrases from the *Useful Language* and *Everyday English* boxes.

CHECK

6 Work with another pair. Listen to their explanation and complete the notes.

How does the object work? ______________________
____

Do you understand how to use it? ______________________
____

WRITING
An Opinion Essay

1 **In what ways has life changed for teenagers in the last 30 years?**

2 **Read the essay. Does it mention any of your ideas in Exercise 1?**

Are teenagers today more or less stressed than previous generations?

The world has changed a great deal in the last few decades, especially for teenagers, and not always in a positive way. In particular, people of my generation are a lot more stressed than teenagers in the past.

First, we are under enormous pressure to do well on exams. This means that we spend a lot of time studying. Young people didn't use to study as much because it wasn't always necessary to go to college. Therefore, they had more time to relax and hang out with friends.

Second, previous generations didn't have online profiles to worry about. In fact, young people 20 or 30 years ago hadn't even heard of "followers" and "likes" because social media hadn't been invented yet. For people of my age, it is almost impossible to do without social media. In addition, it can become extremely addictive.

In conclusion, I would say that teenagers today have more stressful lives than our parents did.

3 **Complete the chart with the linkers from the *Useful Language* box. Look at the linkers in the essay to help you.**

Order of Ideas	Connection Between Ideas
first	

Useful Language

first in addition in conclusion second therefore this means that

4 **Complete the essay with the linkers from the *Useful Language* box. Do you agree with the writer? Sometimes there is more than one possible answer.**

Are online games bad for you?

In my opinion, online games have many good points. [1] First, they improve your memory and your problem-solving skills.

[2] ____________, you can make friends.
[3] ____________, you play with people from around the world. [4] ____________ you often have to communicate in English and [5] ____________ your English improves. However, it's important to spend time with your friends offline.

[6] ____________, online games can be unhealthy, but only if you spend all your time playing them.

PLAN

5 **Write an opinion essay. Look at the statement and take notes in your notebook.**

Teenagers today have more freedom than in the past.

Do you agree or disagree with the statement?

Write two reasons for your opinion.

Give a summary of your opinion.

WRITE

6 **Write your opinion essay. Remember to include *used to*, the simple past and past perfect, and phrases from the *Useful Language* box.**

CHECK

7 **Do you ...**

- give your opinion?
- give reasons for your opinion?
- summarize your opinion?

Finished? p119 Ex. 4

HISTORY PROJECT

1 FASHION

Fashion is always changing, and old styles often come back into fashion, although few people look forward to seeing 1970s fashion again. If you watch TV shows from that decade, you will see that people used to wear pants that were tight at the top and wide at the bottom, flowery dresses, a lot of tight cotton T-shirts or shirts with big collars, and plenty of big round glasses. During the early 1970s, bright colors were extremely trendy, but by the end of the decade they had almost completely disappeared. Black, white, gray, and brown had replaced them, although people still wore enormous glasses.

2 TECHNOLOGY

It is hard to imagine dealing with the ups and downs of modern life without computers and smartphones. However, in the 1970s, there were very few computers, and the ones that existed were a lot bigger than those we have today. They were far slower, with simple displays and enormous buttons. Compared to the devices we use today, they also had very little memory. In fact, the computers on the Apollo spaceships that took men to the moon had less memory than some modern toasters. By the beginning of the 1970s, some companies had started to use computers in their offices, but it was extremely rare to see a computer in a house. In fact, most people had never used one, and some people had never seen one.

A History Exhibition

1 **Look at the photos. What period in history do you think they are from?**

2.13 2 **Read the exhibit labels. Which one do you find most interesting? Why?**

3 **Complete the chart about exhibits 2 and 3.**

	1	2	3
Area	Fashion	Technology	Music
Period	1970s		
Examples	pants (tight at top, wide at bottom), flowery dresses, big glasses, bright colors		
Changes Over Time	black, white, gray, brown became more popular		

3 MUSIC

Music has always been an important part of teenage identity, but in an age of streaming and downloading, it's easy to forget that it hasn't always been as available as it is today. In the 1970s, young music fans would spend hours in record shops looking for new music to buy. It wasn't only the music that was popular. The record covers were also important, and many of them became famous for their artwork. By the middle of the 1990s, CDs had become more popular than records. Nevertheless, people continued to collect records, and DJs still used to play them at dance clubs. Recently, they have come back into style, as many people prefer the sound of a record to the sound of a digital file.

PLAN

4 Make a history exhibition. Work in groups. Complete the steps below.

- Read the tips in *How to Schedule*.
- Decide which period in history you want to concentrate on (for example, the 19th century, the 1980s).
- Choose three areas you want to focus on.

entertainment fashion food and drink house and home school life technology/communication toys and games

- Decide who is going to research and write about which exhibit.

PRESENT

5 Present your history exhibition on a wall of your classroom. Remember to include a title for each label, vocabulary from this unit, *used to*, the simple past and past perfect, and the tips in *How to Schedule*.

CHECK

6 Read the other groups' history exhibitions. What areas are they focusing on? Which group's exhibition is most interesting?

How to Schedule

Ask your teacher how long you have to complete the project. Then decide together how long to spend on each of these stages:

1. looking for information and photos
2. writing draft texts for the labels
3. checking and correcting the drafts
4. writing the final labels and putting them on a poster with the photos

2 REVIEW

VOCABULARY

1 Complete the conversation with the correct form of a phrasal verb.

A How was your bike trip? Where did you go?

B Well, we wanted to [1] ________________ a new route. We were planning to bike to this old town near the ocean, but we got lost and [2] ________________ on a farm!

A Didn't you have a map with you?

B No, but the farmer helped us, so it [3] ________________ OK in the end. We found the town!

A Was it nice there?

B Beautiful. I'd love to [4] ________________ one day. How was your weekend?

A Not great. I was sick. My friends wanted me to go a concert. I'd said yes, and I [5] ________________ to it, but in the end I had to [6] ________________ them ________________.

2 (Circle) the correct words.

Did you know ...?

- The [1]*lids / straps* of plastic water bottles are made from a different plastic than the bottle is.
- If you change the [2]*lens / display* on your phone to black and white, it can become less addictive.
- On old trains, you couldn't open the doors with a [3]*button / plug*. You had to use a [4]*strap / handle*, like a normal door.

GRAMMAR IN ACTION

3 Complete the text with *used to*, *would*, or the simple past and the verb in parentheses. Sometimes there is more than one possible answer.

My dad's a writer now, although he [1] ________________ (not be). He [2] ________________ (be) a diplomat, so my family [3] ________________ (move) all the time. Once, we [4] ________________ (live) in three different countries in two years! I remember when we [5] ________________ (move) to Rio de Janeiro. I [6] ________________ (not know) any Portuguese at first, so the first week [7] ________________ (be) difficult. I used to take my lunch to the playground and then I [8] ________________ (eat) it alone. However, after a few days, my classmates [9] ________________ (start) to invite me to eat with them and I quickly [10] ________________ (make) friends.

4 Complete Diego's message to Tom with the past perfect form of the verbs in parentheses.

Tom, I'm so sorry I missed the wedding! I decided to take the car to the airport, but because I [1] ________________ (never / drive) there before, I got lost. Just the night before, I [2] ________________ (think), "I must leave early!," but then I completely forgot! Anyway, I got to the airport around ten o'clock. The plane [3] ________________ (not taken off), but by the time I finished checking in, the gate [4] ________________ (close). I tried to buy a ticket for the next flight, but they [5] ________________ (already / sell out)!

Self-Assessment

I can use phrasal verbs to talk about changes.

I can talk about parts of objects.

I can use *used to*, *would*, and the simple past.

I can use the past perfect with *never*, *ever*, *already*, *by* (*then*), *by the time*.

LEARN TO LEARN

LEARN TO ... HELP YOUR PARTNER IMPROVE THEIR WRITING

When you write something, ask your partner to check it. You can improve your writing this way.

1 **Read the instructions for the writing task. Correct Edison's mistakes to help him improve.**

WRITING TASK

Write about a favorite toy or game from your childhood.

- Write between 100 and 130 words.
- Use language from this unit.

Don't forget to use punctuation and check your spelling!

When I was little, I [1]~~use~~ used to play with Lego® bricks all the time. I would [2]building ________ all kinds of things – cars, [3]airplaynes ________, houses. I even built a computer with keys and a display. After I finished one thing, I would keep it and then try out something else, but I once [4]used to build ________ a ship that I kept for weeks. [5]I've ________ never built anything like it before. However, I remember my mom [6]would be ________ really angry with me one day because I played with it in the bathroom and ended up damaging the sides of the bathtub. I still have a photo of it somewhere [7], ________

Number of words: 107

2 **Answer the questions in the checklist. Has Edison completed the task in Exercise 1?**

Checklist	Edison's Writing	Your Partner's Writing
Has he/she ...		
1 written about the topic?	Yes / No	Yes / No
2 written between 100 and 130 words?	Yes / No	Yes / No
3 used phrasal verbs for changes and words for parts of objects?	Yes / No	Yes / No
4 added details to make it interesting?	Yes / No	Yes / No
How well has he/she used ...		
5 the simple past?	☹ 😐 🙂	☹ 😐 🙂
6 *used to* and *would*?	☹ 😐 🙂	☹ 😐 🙂
7 the past perfect?	☹ 😐 🙂	☹ 😐 🙂
8 punctuation?	☹ 😐 🙂	☹ 😐 🙂
9 correct spelling?	☹ 😐 🙂	☹ 😐 🙂
Other comments?	*I enjoyed the part about your mom being angry!*	

SHAPE IT!

3 **Do the writing task in Exercise 1.**

4 **Answer the questions in the checklist for your partner's writing.**

5 **Tell your partner what you like and what they can improve.**

3 What's usually on your plate?

LEARNING OUTCOMES

I can ...

- understand texts from an online forum and a cooking show
- give cooking instructions
- write a listicle
- understand how to use different future forms
- talk about cooking and quantities
- make adjectives from verbs, use diagrams, understand words from context by using the rest of the text, and set and achieve learning goals

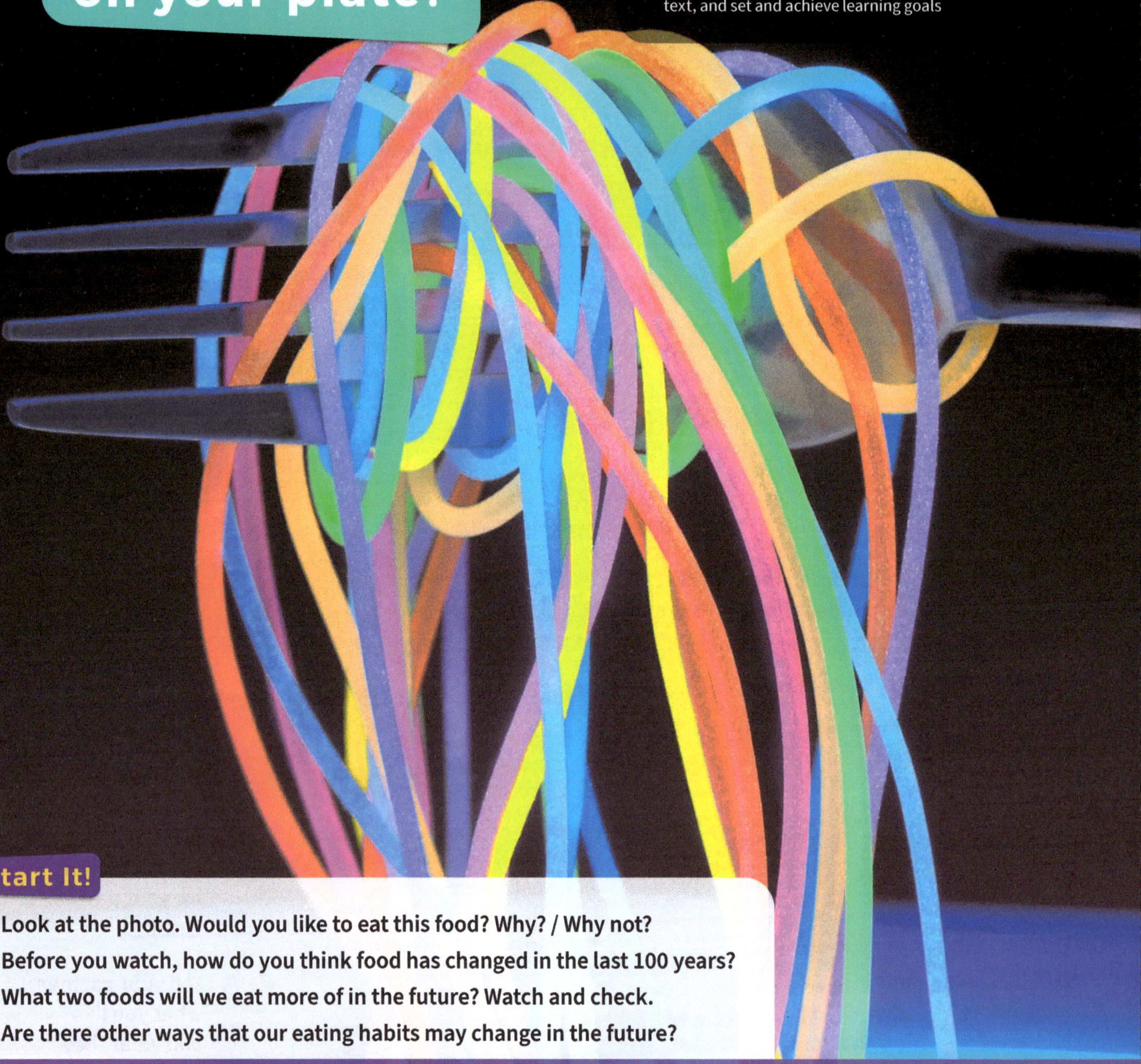

Start It!

1 Look at the photo. Would you like to eat this food? Why? / Why not?
2 Before you watch, how do you think food has changed in the last 100 years?
3 What two foods will we eat more of in the future? Watch and check.
4 Are there other ways that our eating habits may change in the future?

Watch video 3.1

p37

Grammar in Action 3.2

p39

Grammar in Action 3.3

p40

Everyday English 3.4

p42

Globetrotters 3.5

VOCABULARY

Cooking Verbs

1 3.01 **Match the verbs in the box with photos 1–12. Then listen, check, and repeat.**

bake	1	grate		roast	
boil		grill		season	
chop		overcook		slice	
fry		peel		spread	

2 3.02 **Circle the correct verbs to complete the instructions for making a homemade pizza. Then listen and check.**

[1]*Spread* / *Boil* the tomatoes and [2]*peel* / *grate* them. Then [3]*spread* / *chop* them into small pieces, put them in a pan, and [4]*spread* / *season* them with herbs and garlic. [5]*Slice* / *Roast* some bread. Then [6]*fry* / *spread* the tomatoes on the bread and [7]*grate* / *season* some cheese on top. [8]*Fry* / *Bake* it in the oven, but only for a few minutes – you don't want to [9]*overcook* / *peel* it!

3 **Circle the verb that does not go with each food.**

1 pepper:	chop	fry	spread
2 bread:	bake	roast	slice
3 chicken:	boil	overcook	grate
4 fish:	peel	grill	season

LEARN TO LEARN

Wordbuilding: Adjectives from Verbs

Learn the adjective form of new verbs. Sometimes the form is similar, for example, *bake* (v), *baked* (adj).

4 **Write the adjective forms of the verbs. Check your answers with a dictionary.**

bake baked	overcook ______
boil ______	peel ______
chop ______	roast ______
fry ______	season ______
grate ______	slice ______
grill ______	

5 **Which verbs in Exercise 1 usually go with the foods in the box?**

apple bread butter cake carrots cheese chicken egg fish jam orange pasta potatoes spinach steak

You can spread butter or jam on bread. You can have a fried egg.

Use It!

6 **Discuss the questions.**

1 Do you usually eat boiled, grilled, fried, baked, or roasted foods? Which are your favorites?
2 What can you cook?
3 Is it important to know how to cook? Why?

Explore It!

Guess the correct answer.

During the Chinese mid-autumn festival, people traditionally bake mooncakes. Which ingredient is baked inside them to symbolize the moon?

a chicken egg b ostrich egg c duck egg

Find another fact about a traditional food. Write a question for your partner.

Pronunciation p141

READING
An Online Forum

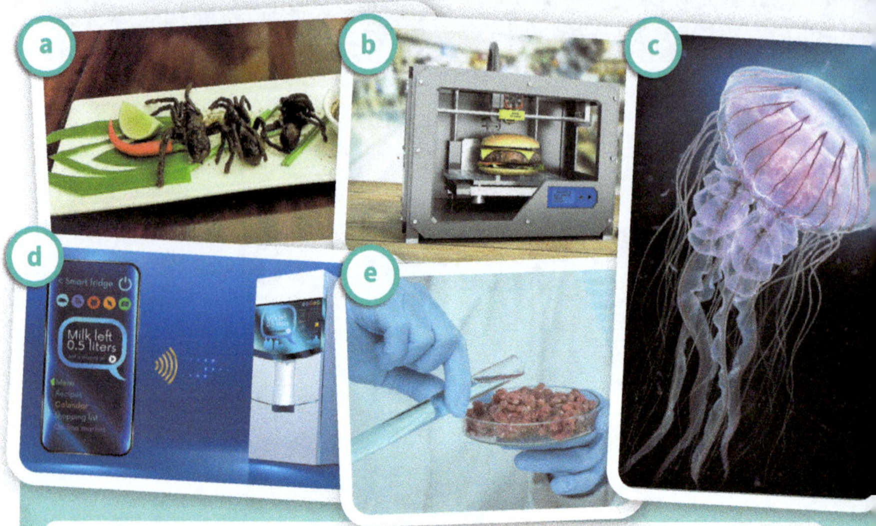

1 **What types of food can you see in the photos? Which ones would you eat?**

3.05 2 **Read the forum and match comments 1–5 with photos a–e.**

3 **Read the forum again and match the future food solutions with the reasons.**

Future Food Solution

1 ☐ jellyfish
2 ☐ lab food
3 ☐ smart fridges
4 ☐ 3-D printers
5 ☐ insects

Why It Solves the Problem

a better for the planet
b can reduce food waste
c a new food and we need these
d cheap and already popular in many places
e healthier and more convenient

4 **Mark (✓) the reasons given for why people might not like future food.**

a unusual in some cultures ☐
b sounds disgusting ☐
c could make humans sick ☐
d not much flavor ☐
e creates new environmental problems ☐

5 **Match the words in bold in the forum with the meanings.**

1 another possibility ____________
2 the taste of something ____________
3 not real ____________
4 something special and good to eat ____________
5 cooking instructions ____________

CLASS 4C STUDY ROOM

Read the article about future food and add your comments. Professor Jones is coming to Friday's class and we're going to discuss your ideas.

1 [c] There isn't going to be enough food for everyone in the future because the population is growing, so we're going to need to be more adventurous and find new foods. I read that we could actually eat jellyfish, although many people won't like the idea. Jellyfish probably doesn't have much **flavor**, but if you season it and roast it, it might be tasty! *Abi*

2 ☐ We may eat **artificial** fish or meat grown in a laboratory in the future. I think the idea sounds disgusting, but scientists say it will be better for the planet. I'm definitely not going to eat lab burgers! *Carlos*

3 ☐ We throw away far too much food, often because we buy more than we need. I read about these cool apps that will tell us what's in the fridge and suggest **recipes** with the food we already have so we don't waste so much. I think they'll be really popular. *Jazmin*

4 ☐ One thing I'm not sure about is 3-D printed food. The idea that a printer will produce our food is a little strange. But people say it will be healthier and more convenient, and it might reduce pollution from transporting food products. *Marco*

5 ☐ Experts say that meat will be far more expensive in the future, so we're going to have to eat **alternative** types of food. Insects are cheaper than farm animals, so they may be a solution. Roasted grasshoppers are a popular snack in Mexico and fried tarantulas are a **delicacy** in Cambodia. In fact, a lot of cultures eat bugs, so why can't we? *Emma*

Voice It!

6 **Discuss the questions.**

1 Which of the ideas in the forum are your most and least favorite? Why?
2 What other future food solutions can you think of?

Finished? p120 Ex. 1

GRAMMAR IN ACTION

Future Forms

Watch video 3.2
What's happening this Saturday?
Which workshop might he go to?

Present Tenses and *Be Going To* for Future Plans and Intentions
Friday's class **starts** at nine o'clock.
Professor Jones [1] ___ **coming** to Friday's class
and we**'re** [2] ___ discuss your ideas.

1 **Complete the examples in the chart above. Use the online forum on page 36 to help you.**

Get It Right!

We use the simple present for scheduled events in the future.

The movie starts at two o'clock. **NOT** ~~*The movie is starting at two o'clock.*~~

2 **Circle the correct words to complete the conversation.**

A [1]*Do you / Are you going to* watch the final tonight?

B Yeah. Kate [2]*comes / is coming* to my house to watch it.

A What time [3]*does it start / is it starting*?

B At 8 p.m., but she [4]*comes / is going to come* at 7 p.m.

Predictions with *Be Going To*, *Will*, and *May*/*Might*
The population is growing, so we [1] _'re going to_ need to find new foods. (a future prediction based on evidence)
We [2] ___ /**might** eat artificial fish or meat. (a future prediction we are not certain about)
Experts say that meat [3] ___ be far more expensive in the future. (a prediction we are certain about)

3 **Complete the examples in the chart above. Use the online forum on page 36 to help you.**

4 **Read the pamphlet. Complete the conversation with the simple present, present continuous, *be going to*, *will*, or *may*/*might* form of the verbs in parentheses.**

Come and have dinner in total darkness, Tuesday to Saturday, 8–10 p.m. Use your other senses to taste the food. Try new, unknown foods and guess what you're eating.

LUCAS Hey Milena, [1] _are_ you _coming_ (come) to Abi's birthday tomorrow?

MILENA Where [2] ___ you ___ (go)?

LUCAS To "Dining in the Dark." We [3] ___ (have) dinner in total darkness!

MILENA That's strange. Abi [4] ___ (not like) it!

LUCAS I'm sure she [5] ___ (love) it! It [6] ___ (be) different from anything she's done before.

MILENA But you [7] ___ (not be able to) see the food. You [8] ___ (eat) something you don't like.

LUCAS I know! We [9] ___ (have to) guess what we're eating!

MILENA What time [10] ___ it ___ (start)?

LUCAS At eight o'clock.

MILENA I'm not sure. I [11] ___ (come). I [12] ___ (tell) you later.

Use It!

5 **Write the questions. Use future forms. Then ask and answer.**

1 What / you / do / tomorrow?
What are you going to do tomorrow?

2 How old / you / be / in 2050?
___

3 What foods we / eat / in the future?
___

4 When / your next class / start?
___

What are you going to do tomorrow?

I'm not sure. I might go to the beach.

Finished? p120 Ex. 2

VOCABULARY AND LISTENING
Quantities

3.06 **1 Read the recipe and choose the correct photo 1–3. Then listen and repeat.**

1 

2 

3 

How to Make Your Own Fruity Cereal

Mix the following ingredients in a bowl:

- a **cup of** cereal, like oats
- some **pieces of** strawberry
- some **slices of** banana
- some **chunks of** pineapple
- a **handful of** blueberries
- a **bag of** nuts
- a **pinch of** cinnamon
- a **sprinkle of** brown sugar

Serve with a **spoonful of** yogurt or a **splash of** milk.

Nutritious and delicious!

2 Complete the sentences with quantities from the recipe from Exercise 1 in the singular or plural form.

1 I have two _slices_ of toast for breakfast and coffee with __________ milk.
2 If your throat hurts, have __________ honey.
3 Season the pasta sauce with __________ salt and pepper.
4 I'm going to have a __________ of chips for lunch.
5 I love cookies with big __________ chocolate!
6 I make the best Greek salad. I put in __________ of olives, some __________ of feta cheese, and __________ oregano on top.

LEARN TO LEARN
Using Diagrams

Use diagrams to help remember new phrases.

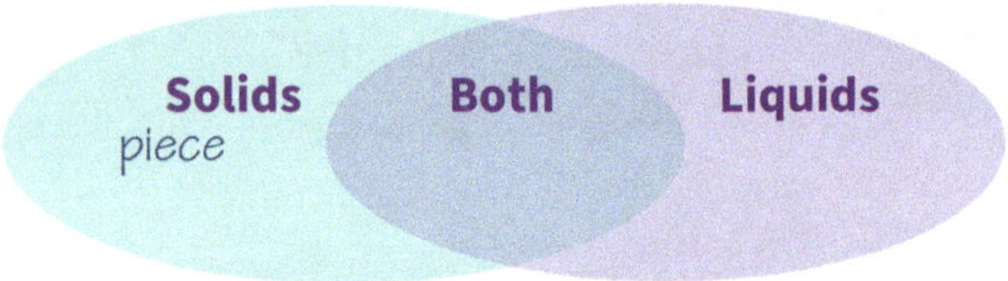

3 Add quantities in Exercise 1 to the diagram in your notebook.

Use it!

4 Think of a food you like and tell your partner the ingredients.

Pancakes ... You need two cups of flour ...

A Recipe

3.07 **5 Listen to the cooking show and write the quantities.**

Pear Smoothie	Ant Tacos
1 __________ orange juice	6 __________ ant larvae
2 __________ chopped pear	7 __________ chopped tomatoes
3 __________ cricket flour	8 __________ chopped chilies
4 __________ mango and pineapple	9 __________ salt and pepper
5 __________ lime juice	10 __________ chopped cilantro

3.07 **6 Listen again and circle the correct answers.**

1 Both of Anton's dishes ....
  a contain insects. c are Mexican.
  b are spicy.
2 By 2030 there will be ... billion people in the world.
  a 5.5 b 6.5 c 8.5
3 Cricket flour will add ... to the smoothie.
  a fruit flavor b vitamins c protein
4 Anton is going to ... the ant larvae.
  a fry b boil c roast

Watch video 3.3
Who will be making our food in the future?
What food was invented by accident?

GRAMMAR IN ACTION

Future Continuous and Future Perfect

	Future Continuous	Future Perfect
+	I [1] will be making a pear smoothie.	We [4] ______ **tasted** some very unusual dishes.
–	I [2] ______ **adding** milk or yogurt.	They [5] ______ **cooked** in time.
?	What [3] ______ you ______ **making** today?	[6] ______ you ______ **finished** by the end of the show?

1 Complete the examples in the chart above with ***will/won't be*** or ***will/won't have***.

2 Complete the sentences with the future continuous form of the verbs in the box.

eat	not see	stay	~~sleep~~

1 Don't call me at 8:30. I'll be sleeping.
2 Where ______ they ______ while they're on vacation?
3 I have exams next week. I ______ my friends.
4 ______ we ______ insects in 30 years?

3 Complete the sentences with the future perfect form of the verbs in parentheses.

1 I think scientists will have found (find) life on other planets by 2060.
2 I ______ ______ (not finish) my exams by the end of May.
3 They ______ (not start) yet. It's only 7:30.

3.08 **4** Complete the conversation with the future continuous or future perfect form of the verbs in parentheses. Then listen and check.

ZOE How [1] will restaurants have changed (change) by 2030?
SAM I think they [2] ______ (become) more automatic. Instead of human chefs, machines [3] ______ (cook) your food and human waiters [4] ______ (not serve) the tables, robots will.
ZOE So humans [5] ______ (not work) in restaurants?
SAM That's right, but I think we [6] ______ (design) robots that look like humans by then.

Use It!

5 Write sentences about your future. Use the future continuous or future perfect and the phrases in the box.

In one year … In 2050 …
On my 21st birthday …
By the end of this year … By 2030 …
By the time I'm 25 …

In 2050, I'll be living in my own house.
By the time I'm 25, I'll have learned how to drive.

6 Tell your partner your sentences about the future, but change some so that they are false. Can they guess which sentences are true and which are false?

In 2050, I won't be living in my own house.

False?

Yes, it's false.

Finished? p120 Ex. 3

SPEAKING
Giving Instructions

3.09 **1 What can you see in the photo? What ingredients do you need to make it? Listen and check your answers.**

JOE Can you give me the recipe for your tasty Spanish omelet? I'm going to make it for the picnic tomorrow. It won't take forever, will it?

AMY No, it's a piece of cake! [1] You'll need two cooked potatoes, five eggs, salt, oil, and an onion.

JOE

AMY

JOE OK. Is that it?

AMY Yep, so [2] ____________ slicing the potatoes. [3] ____________ chop the onion.

JOE OK. Then what?

AMY Heat half a cup of oil in a pan and fry the potatoes and onions.

JOE That's a good bit of oil!

AMY Yeah, I know! [4] ____________ frying, mix the eggs in a bowl. Then put everything together and add a pinch of salt. Heat a spoonful of oil in a smaller pan and pour in the mixture. Once the bottom part has cooked, [5] ____________ flip the omelet and cook the other side.

JOE OK, I'll try.

AMY It's delicious! Your friends will all be asking for the recipe! Will you still be there at four?

JOE Yeah, but we'll have finished the omelet by then!

3.09 **2 Complete the conversation with the phrases from the *Useful Language* box. Then listen again and check.**

Useful Language

don't forget to … (+ verb) Once that's done, …
start by … (+ *-ing*) While that's … (+ *-ing*)
You'll need …

3 Match the words and phrases (1–4) with the words and phrases in the *Everyday English box*. How do you say these phrases in your language?

1 something that's easy
2 delicious
3 Is that everything?
4 a long time

Watch video 3.4
Everyday English

a piece of cake ☐ forever ☐
Is that it? ☐ tasty ☐

PLAN

4 Write about a recipe and the ingredients you need.

____

____

____

SPEAK

5 Practice explaining the recipe to your partner. Remember to use future forms, vocabulary from this unit, and phrases from the *Useful Language* and *Everyday English* boxes.

CHECK

6 Work with another pair. Listen to their conversation and complete the notes.

What was the recipe for? ____________

____

What ingredients do you need?

____

____

Would you like to eat this food?

____

WRITING
A Listicle

1 **What food can you see in the photos? Read Megan's listicle. Which of her predictions do you agree with?**

2 **The following are features of a good listicle. Which ones are in Megan's listicle?**

1 an interesting title
2 a number in the title
3 short texts about the title, one for each number
4 some interesting predictions
5 photos

FIVE FOODS WE'LL ALL BE EATING IN 2070!

1 If there's one thing we'll still be eating in 50 years, it's pizza!
We've been eating pizza since the 19th century, so we're not going to stop now! In the future, toppings will change for sure, but pizza isn't going anywhere!

2 Tasty meat alternatives
With more humans on the planet, we'll need alternative sources of protein, such as insects. What could be tastier than a sprinkle of roasted ants on your salad?

3 Classics that will never die out!
Some classic British dishes, like fish and chips, will be around forever, although the fish will probably come from fish farms instead of the ocean.

4 Printed snacks
By 2070, we'll be printing most of our snacks with a 3-D printer. Impossible? Watch this space ...

5 Vegetarians and vegans
Vegetarian food is here to stay! In 2070 being vegetarian or vegan, and avoiding eggs, milk, and cheese, will be the norm!

3 **Read Megan's listicle again and make two lists.**

Food That Will Be the Same	Food That Will Be New
pizza	

4 **Complete the *Useful Language* phrases with the words in the box. Check in Megan's listicle.**

anywhere forever norm space stay

Useful Language

is here to [1] ____________
isn't going [2] ____________
Watch this [3] ____________
will be around [4] ____________
will be the [5] ____________

PLAN

5 **Write your own listicle. Look at the questions and take notes.**

What will people still be eating in 50 years?
____

What might we start eating in the future?
____

Which dishes will be around forever?
____

What food is unusual now but will be normal in the future?
____

WRITE

6 **Write a listicle about your future food predictions. Remember to include future forms, vocabulary from this unit, and phrases from the *Useful Language* box.**

CHECK

7 **Do you ...**

- explain what we will or might be eating in the future?
- explain what will be normal in the future?
- make any other predictions?

Finished? p120 Ex. 4

AROUND THE WORLD

READING
An Article

3.10 **1** **Look at the photos. What can you see? What do they tell you about food in Australia? Read the article and check your ideas.**

Globetrotters

Watch video 3.5
Food in Japan

- What food is usually associated with your country or culture?
- Can you explain what *kaiseki* and *wagashi* are?
- How is Western food influencing Japanese food traditions?

Voice It!

2 **Discuss the questions.**

1 People need to be open-minded to eat foods from other cultures or to change ways of getting food. How have people in Australia been open-minded about food?

2 What are the benefits of being open-minded about food?

3 How open-minded are you?

A TASTE OF *Australia*

A country's food is influenced by its inhabitants, geography, climate, and wildlife, and Australia is no exception.

Traditional Australia

For thousands of years, the indigenous people of Australia have eaten plants and animals from the land or ocean. Traditional Aboriginal food, or "bush tucker," includes crocodile, emu, and snake. Examples that are still eaten today include kangaroo, macadamia nuts, and witchetty grubs. These tasty insect larvae are roasted on the fire or grilled on the barbecue!

Multicultural Australia

Since the first Europeans arrived in Australia over 200 years ago, people have been moving to the country from all over the world. As a result, Australian cuisine is multicultural and includes British, Italian, Greek, and Asian food. Popular dishes are fish and chips, roasted lamb, and dim sum, as well as traditional favorites such as kangaroo, seafood pizza, and fried shark. The warm, sunny climate means plenty of fresh fruit and vegetables and barbecues to grill meat or fish outside.

Tomorrow's Australia

Desert Food

Australia has built the first farm in the world that can grow fruit and vegetables in a desert. The enormous solar-powered greenhouse only needs sunshine and seawater to work, and Australia has plenty of both. The solar panels create enough energy to transform the saltwater into fresh water, which is used to water the tomato plants. It's strange to think that in the future we might be eating food that is grown in the desert.

Ugly Food

Around a quarter of the fruit and vegetables around the world is thrown away before it gets to the supermarkets because people believe it's too "ugly" to sell. However, some Australian supermarkets are trying to sell this food. They tell their customers that even though the food looks odd, it tastes exactly the same as perfectly formed fruit and vegetables. There are a lot of advantages to eating this ugly food. It's less expensive for customers, farmers sell more of their produce, and we reduce food waste.

LEARN TO LEARN

Understanding Words from Context

When you see new words, use the rest of the sentence to help you understand them. Guess what the new word means and then check it in a dictionary.

3 **Find the words in the article and guess the meaning. Then check in a dictionary or with your teacher.**

New Word	What the Other Words Tell Me	What I Think It Means
indigenous	*It's an adjective that describes people who have lived in Australia for a long time.*	*original, first*
witchetty grubs		
multicultural		
shark		
solar-powered		
greenhouse		

4 **Find words in the article that mean …**

1 something not included in a group (introduction). ______________
2 delicious (traditional Australia). ______________
3 a style of cooking (multicultural Australia). ______________
4 strange (ugly food). ______________

Explore It!

Guess the correct answer.

What will you not find on a pizza in Australia?

a emu b kangaroo c koala d crocodile

Find another fact about Australian food. Write a question for your partner to answer.

SHAPE IT!

CULTURE PROJECT

A Poster

A poster presents information about a topic in a visually interesting way. Make a poster about a type of food from around the world.

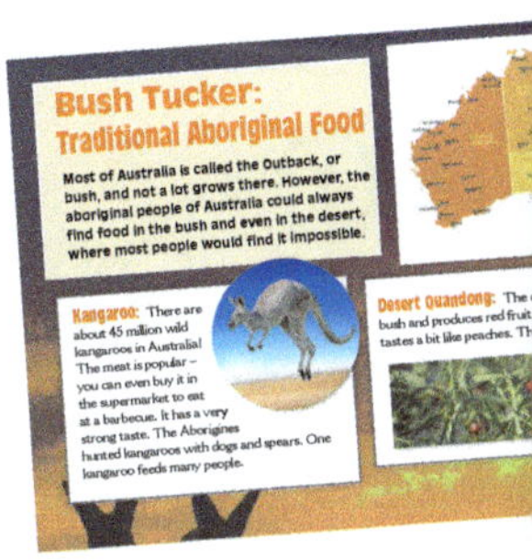

Teacher's Resource Bank

3 REVIEW

VOCABULARY

1 Circle the correct verbs.

1. *Season* / *Peel* the orange before you eat it.
2. Is there any butter to *spread* / *grate* on my toast?
3. Let's *roast* / *fry* a chicken in the oven.
4. Can I borrow a knife to *grill* / *slice* the tomato?
5. Jose *bakes* / *chops* his own bread. It's great!

2 Match the quantities with the photos. Then think of another example for each quantity.

bag	☐	________	pinch	☐	________
chunk	☐	________	slice	☐	________
cup	☐	________	splash	☐	________
handful	☐	________	spoonful	☐	________

1

2

3

4

5

6

7

8

GRAMMAR IN ACTION

3 Circle the correct words to complete the conversation.

MAURO What [1]*do you* / *are you going to* do this afternoon?

ANDREA We [2]*'re going* / *will go* to the movies. Juan and Allie [3]*come* / *are coming*, too.

MAURO What movie [4]*are you going to* / *will you* see?

ANDREA *The Scream Factor.*

MAURO But you hate horror movies!

ANDREA I know! [5]*I'm not enjoying* / *I'm not going to enjoy* the movie, but Allie wants to see it.

MAURO It [6]*might be* / *is* OK. Who knows, you [7]*won't* / *may* enjoy it.

ANDREA We'll see. Anyway, I have to go. It [8]*will start* / *starts* in 45 minutes.

4 Complete the predictions with the future continuous or future perfect form of the verbs in parentheses. Which predictions do you agree / disagree with?

In 10 years …

1. Ethiopian cuisine ________ (become) popular.
2. most people ________ (stop) eating meat.
3. we ________ (not buy) "ugly" fruit and vegetables.
4. we ________ (not go out) to restaurants. We ________ (order) food online to eat at home.

Self-Assessment

I can talk about food preparation.

I can talk about quantities of food.

I can use future forms to talk about plans, intentions, and predictions.

I can use the future continous and future perfect.

LEARN TO LEARN

LEARN TO ... SET AND ACHIEVE LEARNING GOALS

When you know what your English learning goals are, you can take steps to achieve them.

1 **Read what Ada says about her learning goal. What is it? Has she achieved it yet?**

In three weeks, I'm going to New Zealand with my brother. He doesn't speak English, so I'll need to book the hotels, order food, and ask directions. My goal is to learn enough travel English to do this. I've bought a book with useful phrases for tourists, and I've downloaded episodes of a podcast about New Zealand. I'm going to listen to one episode every week. I'm also going to learn one useful phrase from the book every day. Piece of cake!

2 **Write Ada's answers to questions 2–4 in her action plan.**

3 **Read what Enzo says about his learning goal. Write his answers to questions 1 and 2 in his action plan.**

One month from now we have a speaking exam. I want to get a good grade, but I'm not great at speaking – not like my sister. She speaks English really well!

4 **Whose advice should Enzo take?**

Why don't you practice with your sister? Ten minutes a day would help. **Ela**

I'd study a lot of vocabulary the night before. And don't sleep! **Hamid**

Look at the Everyday English phrases in our book. Use three of them every day. **Olga**

5 **Use your answers in Exercise 4 to complete questions 3 and 4 of Enzo's action plan. Write one sentence about his goal for question 5.**

SHAPE IT!

6 **Think of an English learning goal. What are your answers to questions 1 to 5?**

7 **Tell your partner about your learning goal. Use the action plan to help you.**

Action Plan		NAME: Ada	NAME: Enzo
1	What do I want to do?	learn enough travel English to book hotels, order food, and ask directions learn enough travel English	
2	How much time do I have?		
3	How am I going to do it?	a b	a b
4	How often am I going to do the things in 3?	a b	a b
5	What's my goal in one sentence?	By the time we go to New Zealand, I'll have learned enough travel English.	

4 How do you use your senses?

LEARNING OUTCOMES

I can ...

- understand texts about people who don't feel pain or fear, and artists who make sound effects
- make guesses and give clues about unfamiliar objects
- write an encyclopedia entry
- make deductions and express obligation, prohibition, necessity, and advice
- talk about senses and describe how things look, sound, and feel, etc.
- brainstorm, use visual clues when listening, and plan my homework
- create an infographic.

Start It!

1 Look at the photo. What different senses do you use when you go to the beach?
2 Before you watch, what do you think bats, dolphins, and submarines have in common?
3 Which animal has the best hearing and how does that help them? Watch and check.
4 Can you think of any other animals that have special senses?

Watch video 4.1

p49

Grammar in Action 4.2

p51

Grammar in Action 4.3

p52

Everyday English 4.4

VOCABULARY
The Five Senses

1 Match the words in bold with photos A–E. Answer the questions.

Have you ever …

1 seen a **durian**? [ ]
2 touched a **snake**? [ ]
3 played soccer on **artificial grass**? [ ]
4 heard a **koala**? [ ]
5 eaten a **banana split**? [ ]

2 Match the questions in Exercise 1 with statements a–e. Which things did you already know?

a They **look like** friendly teddy bears, but when they cry they **sound** really angry. [4]
b It's made of plastic, but it can often **feel like** the real thing. [ ]
c It **tastes** sweet and it looks really colorful, and it **sounds like** a great idea for a dessert! [ ]
d They **look** wet and slimy, but when you **touch** their skin they **feel** cold and dry. [ ]
e They **smell** terrible. In fact, they **smell like** dirty old socks and they don't **taste like** fruit, but many people say they're delicious. [ ]

LEARN TO LEARN
Brainstorming

Brainstorming word groups can help you make vocabulary connections.

3 Complete each line with the words in bold from Exercise 2. Add three or more words or phrases that you associate with them.

a the ears: sound, sounds like, hear, listen to, music
b the eyes: ____________
c the hands: ____________
d the nose: ____________
e the tongue: ____________

4 Choose one group of words in Exercise 3. Say your extra words to your partner. Can they guess which group they belong to?

5 Complete the sentences with the correct form of words in bold from Exercise 2.

1 When my dad sleeps, he snores so much he sounds like a trumpet!
2 I tried some crocodile meat once. It ____________ chicken.
3 The milk ____________ bad and ____________ a bit yellow, so she didn't taste it.
4 I love wearing my new winter coat. It ____________ so soft and warm.
5 A It ____________ a painting by Picasso.
B No, but it is.
6 Please ____________ the wall. I've just painted it.

Use It!

6 Talk about the things in the box with words from Exercise 2. Compare with another pair. Do you have the same descriptions?

cell phones	fast food	graffiti	new clothes	rap music

Explore It!

Guess the correct answer.

Which human sense is the weakest?

a sight
b hearing
c touch
d taste
e smell

Find another interesting fact about the human senses. Write a question for your partner to answer.

READING

A Magazine Article

1 **Imagine you couldn't feel pain or fear. Would your life be better or worse? Why?**

4.01 2 **Read the magazine article. Which problems does it mention?**

No Pain, No Fear – NO WAY!

Everybody knows what pain feels like. It's horrible. So imagine never feeling physical pain. You cut your finger – nothing. You break your leg – no pain at all. It must be wonderful, right? Wrong, because pain is the body's way of telling the brain that there's a problem. But some people, like Amy Campbell, can't feel pain. When she was born, Amy looked like an ordinary baby, but after a few months, her parents realized something was wrong and thought she had developmental problems. She would chew her tongue and bite her fingers, but she never cried. By the time she was a teenager, she had broken both arms and a leg – all without feeling a thing. It also doesn't matter if the air feels hot or cold, Amy can't feel the weather. But, like any young person, she has friends, hobbies (she plays the guitar), dreams, and ambitions. She just has to be very careful. You may think her life can't be easy, but Amy is optimistic about her future. She says her condition affects what she can do but not who she is inside.

Jordy Cernik

When Jordy Cernik tells people he feels no fear, they usually think he can't be serious. Having no fear might sound like a joke, but it's not. During his 20s and 30s, Jordy had to have operations to remove his adrenal glands. Some time later, he realized that these operations had had a strange effect – he couldn't feel any fear. He did a parachute jump but didn't feel scared at all. He finds rollercoasters boring. Some people imagine it must be great not to feel fear, but there are disadvantages to not having any adrenaline. Adrenaline is a natural painkiller, so Jordy now feels more pain than ordinary people. It also means he doesn't feel excited about anything. Jordy now does "scary" challenges to raise money for charity. Doctors think he could be the only person in the world who feels no fear, but knowledge about his condition may help them understand more common problems like anxiety.

3 EXAM **Choose the correct option.**

1 Pain is important because it tells the brain
- A you're all right.
- B there's a problem.
- C to go to the doctor.
- D to do scary things.

2 Amy Campbell and Jordy Cernik are examples of people who
- A experience life differently.
- B feel no pain.
- C feel no fear.
- D feel no pain or fear.

3 Fear and physical pain
- A prevent us from enjoying life.
- B are only feelings.
- C are always bad.
- D are necessary.

4 **Find words in the article that mean …**

1 to bite something many times with your teeth (Amy). ________

2 the things you want to achieve (Amy). ________

3 a chemical produced by the body (Jordy). ________

4 a chemical or drug that stops pain (Jordy). ________

5 the feeling of being very worried (Jordy). ________

Voice It!

5 **Why do people enjoying doing things like riding on rollercoasters?**

Finished? p121 Ex. 1

GRAMMAR IN ACTION

Modals of Deduction and Possibility

Watch video 4.2
Why is Andy an amazing athlete? How does he know when he's near the edge of the pool?

100% Certain	It [1] _must_ **be** wonderful.
Possible	Having no fear [2] ______ **sound like** a joke, but it's not. Knowledge about his condition [3] ______ **help** them understand more common problems. Doctors think he [4] ______ **be** the only person in the world who feels no fear.
100% Impossible	He [5] ______ **be** serious.

1 Complete the examples in the chart above. Use the magazine article on page 48 to help you.

4.02 **2 Circle the correct words. Then listen and check.**

1 This drink *must* / *can't* have a lot of sugar in it. It tastes really sweet.
2 Don't touch that snake! It *might* / *can't* be poisonous.
3 This milk *must* / *can't* be really old. It smells disgusting.
4 It looks like a painting by Monet, but it *may* / *can't* be. It was painted after he died.
5 A What instrument is that? It sounds like a violin.
  B Maybe, or it *can't* / *could* be a viola.
6 This jacket *must* / *can't* be very warm in winter. It feels like a blanket!

4.03 **3 Complete the conversation with *must*, *can't*, or *might*. Then listen and check.**

MARTÍN What are you listening to? It's so loud!
LIZ It's Beethoven. I think it's beautiful.
MARTÍN You [1] _must_ be joking! I thought you hated classical music.
LIZ Well, that's because I hadn't really listened to any before. Did you know Beethoven became deaf when he was still really young?
MARTÍN Wow, that [2] ______ be easy for anyone, but it [3] ______ be absolutely terrible for a musician. You should turn it down, though. The neighbors [4] ______ be home.
LIZ They [5] ______ be. The lights are off and their car's not there. Anyway, I'm sure they'd prefer Beethoven to the heavy metal you always play. They [6] ______ hate that! Every time you put it on they start banging on the wall.

4 Write sentences about this situation with the verbs and phrases in the boxes. Use *must*, *can't*, *may*, *might*, or *could*.

Marco hasn't come to school yet. He has to give a presentation with his partner, Alice, and all their notes are in Marco's locker.

be	come	feel	have

a cold	in bed	late	nervous
soon	very relaxed	worried	

Marco might be in bed. Alice must feel worried.
______
______
______

Use It!

5 Look at the photos. What do you think they are?

It could/might/can't/must be ...

It looks like (a) ...

1
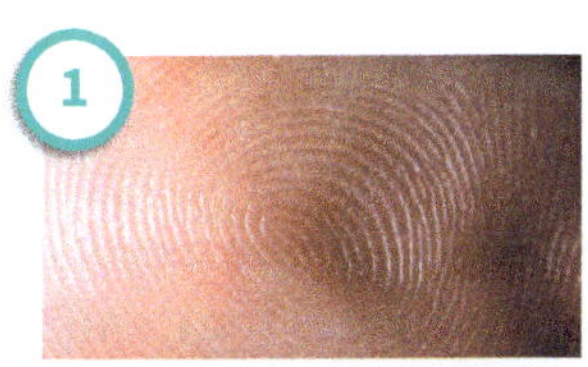

2

3

4

Finished? p121 Ex. 2

VOCABULARY AND LISTENING

Describing Texture, Sound, Taste, Etc.

1 a sharp knife

2 a ________ umbrella

3 a ________ chameleon

4 ________ skin

5 a ________ chili pepper

6 a ________ road

7 a ________ grapefruit

8 ________ balloons

9 a ________ skunk

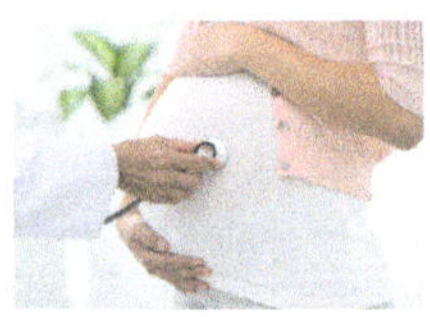
10 a ________ heartbeat

4.04 **1 Complete the photo labels with the words in the box. Then listen, check, and repeat.**

colorful faint rough ~~sharp~~ shiny smelly smooth sour spicy transparent

2 In your notebooks, complete the chart with the words from Exercise 1.

Feel	Look	Smell	Sound	Taste
	colorful			

Use It!

3 Use words in Exercise 1 to describe the things in the box. Can your partner guess the item?

a cat's tongue a chili pepper a lemon a magazine a new coin a pencil old shoes stars whisper

It's shiny and silver.

A new coin!

An Interview

4 Foley artists create sound effects for movies. What sound effects do you think these items make?

a 
two coconut halves

b 
shredded newspaper and a plastic bag

c 
cellophane

d 
celery

e 
rice and a metal tray

I think the coconut halves could be the sound of ...

LEARN TO LEARN

Using Visual Clues When Listening

Use photos, instructions, etc., to help you understand what you are hearing.

4.05 **5 Listen to the interview with James Ford, a Foley artist. Were your answers to Exercise 4 correct?**

4.05 **6 Listen again and circle the correct words.**

1 It's important to *never* / *sometimes* have total silence in a movie.
2 The interviewer thinks the second effect is made with *newspaper* / *grass*.
3 Foley artists used to make *more* / *fewer* sounds.
4 James *made some* / *didn't make any* of the explosion sounds in his last movie.
5 To become a Foley artist, formal training is *necessary* / *unnecessary*.

Voice It!

7 Do you think the job of a Foley artist will disappear in the future? Why / Why not?

Watch video 4.3
What is she giving advice about?
What three things do you need to do?

GRAMMAR IN ACTION

Obligation, Prohibition, Necessity, and Advice

	Obligation	Prohibition
+	They **must** sound natural.	
–	These days we [1] don't **have to** make them all.	You **must not** speak loudly in the library.
?	[2] ______ you **have to** work hard?	

	Necessity	Advice
+	We [3] ______ **to** experiment a lot.	We [5] ______ listen to one more effect. You **ought to** practice listening.
–	You **don't need** [4] ______ have any formal training.	You **shouldn't** do that.
?	**Do** you **need to** be creative?	**Should** we listen again?

Pronunciation p141

Past Obligation

In the past, Foley artists [1] ______ create all the effects.
I **didn't** [2] ______ make those sounds.
[3] ______ your parents ______ study English at school?

1 Complete the chart above. Write one word in each blank.

2 Circle the correct words.

7 TIPS FOR TAKING CARE OF YOUR EYES

1. Most of us [1] *must not / need to* use computers every day, but too much screen time can be bad for your eyes.
2. You [2] *ought to / shouldn't* spend more than about 20 minutes looking at a screen without taking a break.
3. You [3] *should / shouldn't* avoid using your phone in the dark. If you want to read, you [4] *ought to / have to* read a book.
4. Some people [5] *don't have to / must not* wear glasses, but if you do, you [6] *should / ought not to* keep the lenses clean.
5. Buy a good pair of sunglasses: everybody [7] *needs to / must not* protect their eyes from bright sunlight.
6. Don't forget about diet, either. It [8] *ought to / must not* include a lot of green vegetables and fatty fish.
7. Finally, everybody [9] *doesn't have to / should* have an eye exam once a year.

3 Complete the chart above with the correct form of *have to*.

Get It Right!
We don't use **must** in the past, only **had to**.

4 Match 1-4 with a-d. Then listen and check. (4.08)

1. She didn't have to study hard for the exam [d]
2. Billy didn't have to get up early this morning [ ]
3. Mia had to go to the dentist [ ]
4. I got all the answers wrong, [ ]

a. because it's a holiday.
b. so I had to do the exercise again.
c. because she had a toothache.
d. because she's really good at English.

5 Complete the text with the correct form of *have to*.

These days most people have a camera on their phone. In the past, you [1] had to be rich to own a camera. When you took a photo, the people [2] ______ stand still. The photographer [3] ______ be careful because photos were expensive. Now, we [4] ______ worry because we can take a ton.

Use It!

6 Take notes and compare with a partner.

- something you had to do in the past
- something you ought to do soon

Finished? p121 Ex. 3

SPEAKING

Making Guesses and Giving Clues

4.09 **1 Look at the photo. What are *tabi*? Listen and find out.**

ED Hey, do you want to see something cool?
ZOE Sure, why not? Wow! What are those?
ED They're called *tabi*. They're from Japan. [1]Guess what they are.
ZOE Well, they're [2]________ of clothing. They look like gloves, but they can't be, can they?
ED Nope. They're definitely not gloves.
ZOE They're in the shape of an "L," so I guess [3]________ socks.
ED Bingo!
ZOE But why is the big toe separate from the other toes?
ED I'm not telling you. Try to figure it out yourself.
ZOE Hmm. Perhaps [4]________ traditional. Maybe Japanese people wear rings on their big toes?
ED No, that's not it. [5]________ again.
ZOE No, I give up!
ED It's so that they can wear them with sandals with straps. The strap goes between the big toe and the others.
ZOE Oh, that's a smart idea! They must be nice and warm to wear.
ED I guess so. I haven't tried them on yet.

4.09 **2 Complete the conversation with phrases from the *Useful Language* box. Then listen again and check.**

Useful Language

Guess again.
Guess what it is / they are.
I guess they must be …
Perhaps it's something (+ *adjective*)
They're definitely some kind of …

3 Complete the conversations with the phrases in the *Everyday English* box.

1 A Want to watch a movie? B ________
2 It's ________ today. Let's have a picnic!
3 A Is the answer 23? B ________
4 A Chinese must be hard to learn. B ________
5 A One more guess? B No – ________

Watch video 4.4
Everyday English

Bingo! I give up! I guess so.
nice and warm/hot, etc. Sure, why not?

PLAN

4 Write about something from your country that might be new or strange to a foreigner, for example, a kind of food or an item of clothing. How would you describe it?

Topic: ________
Description: ________
Purpose: ________

SPEAK

5 Practice describing something from your country to your partner. Remember to use vocabulary from this unit.

CHECK

6 Work with another pair. Listen to their conversation and complete the notes.

What did you hear about? ________
____
How was it described? ________
____

WRITING
An Encyclopedia Entry

1 **Look at the photos. What do you think the thing attached to the man's head does? Read the encyclopedia entry and check your ideas.**

1 ☐ Neil Harbisson was born on July 27, 1984.

2 ☐ Neil Harbisson is known as the world's first cyborg artist. He has been color blind since birth and has a special antenna connected to his skull that lets him "hear" colors as different vibrations in his head.

3 ☐ Neil was born in Belfast and grew up in Barcelona. At the age of 16, he started to make black and white art. In 2004, scientists developed his special camera and attached it to his head. With the camera, Neil can "hear" 360 colors, including some that are invisible to the human eye. In 2004, when he had to get a new passport, the UK passport office said no at first because he didn't look like a human. However, they finally accepted his application. He must be the only official cyborg in the world.

4 ☐ Neil now makes colorful art, including "sound portraits" of famous people and geometric paintings. He has had exhibitions all around the world.

5 ☐ According to Neil, all human skin sounds orange.

2 **Match headings a–e with paragraphs 1–5.**

a Artwork
b Other Information
c Introduction
d Name and Date of Birth
e Life

3 **Are the sentences *T* (true) or *F* (false)?**

1 Neil has always lived in the same place. ___
2 Neil doesn't always wear his antenna. ___
3 Neil can experience colors that ordinary humans can't see. ___
4 Neil couldn't get a new British passport. ___
5 People in many countries have seen Neil's art. ___

4 **Complete the sentences with the phrases from the *Useful Language* box.**

1 Stefani Joanne Angelina Germanotta ________ Lady Gaga.
2 She ________ March 28, 1986 ________ New York City.
3 ________ four she began to learn to play the piano.
4 She makes energetic pop music, ________ songs like *Bad Romance* and *Alejandro*.
5 ________ Lady Gaga, you can teach yourself art.

Useful Language

According to ...	and grew up in ...
At the age of ...	including ...
... is known as ...	... was born on ...

PLAN

5 **These artists all have a physical difference. Choose one and take notes.**

photographer Roesie Percy
chef Adam Cole
rapper Sean Forbes

Name and date of birth: ________

Their life: ________

Their work: ________

WRITE

6 **Write your encyclopedia entry. Remember to include five paragraphs, vocabulary from this unit, and phrases from the *Useful Language* box.**

CHECK

7 **Do you ...**

- include information about the person's life?
- include information about the person's work?

Finished? p121 Ex. 4

SCIENCE PROJECT

An Infographic

1 Work in pairs. Can you answer the questions?

1. Which continents do elephants live on?
2. How do they know where they are going?
3. How strong is their trunk (their long nose)?
4. What do they use their ears for?

2 Read the infographic and check your answers to Exercise 1.

How to Research

3 Which of these things should you do when you research? Mark (✓) the correct answers.

1. Decide the main information you want before doing research. ✓
2. Use questions in search engines, e.g., *How well can elephants see?* ☐
3. Read articles from start to finish. ☐
4. Read the contents list of articles or the titles of sections and then decide what you need to read. ☐
5. Make sure the information is fact and not opinion. ☐
6. Only check information on one site. ☐
7. Take notes as you read. ☐

Elephants and

Elephants' eyes are on the side of their head and have three eyelids, one above the eye and one below, like humans, and an almost transparent one they use to keep dust, dirt, and water out. However, their eyes aren't very strong. They normally use their trunks to know where they are going. In fact, the leader of a group of elephants is sometimes blind.

Elephants can hear extremely well because they have big ears. They can hear faint sounds, including the calls of elephants up to 1.5 km away. Their ears are about $1/6$ of the size of their bodies. They also use them to keep cool.

Elephants have to move their trunk around and smell the air all the time in order to find water, so they have an excellent sense of smell. They can detect water up to 12 km away.

Elephants use their rough trunks to explore the environment and care for their young. They also use them to fight. The trunk can lift objects that weigh up to 250 kg. They can also sense tiny vibrations in the ground with their feet. Scientists think this must be the reason why many survived the Asian Tsunami of 2004. They felt the vibrations of the earthquake and moved to higher ground.

SHAPE IT!

Their **Amazing** Senses

- Two species: African and Asian
- Males: 2,700 to 6,300 kg
- Females: 1,800 to 3,600 kg
- Lifespan: approx. 65 years
- 100,000 muscles in the trunk

PLAN

4 Work in groups to make an infographic. Choose an animal you want to research. Decide who is going to research which sense. Remember to:

- use the tips in *How to* Research
- have a title for your infographic
- use photos
- make the headings and the contents easy to read
- use numbers (21, ⅔, etc.) instead of words (twenty-one, two-thirds).

PRESENT

5 Present your infographic to your class. Remember to include interesting facts, visuals, and headings, and vocabulary from this unit.

CHECK

6 Look at the other groups' infographics. Tell the group members which information you find most interesting.

4 REVIEW

VOCABULARY

1 Complete the sentences with the correct sense verb.

1 A Do you ________________ your mom or your dad?
  B My mom – I have the same eyes as her.
2 This coffee ________________ incredibly sweet.
3 Your perfume ________________ roses.
4 Your forehead ________________ hot, Dan. You might have a fever.
5 Listen! Do you hear that noise? It ________________ a mouse.
6 Ouch! I ________________ a cactus!
7 I've just started to learn the guitar. I ________________ very good yet, but one day I will.

2 Circle the correct words.

1 I don't like *spicy* / *smooth* food much – it burns my mouth.
2 I heard a very *transparent* / *faint* sound in the distance.
3 Are they new shoes? They're so *smelly* / *shiny* – I love them!
4 Be careful with that knife! It's really *sharp* / *faint*.
5 The pictures in that book are really *sour* / *colorful*.
6 These glasses are not completely *smelly* / *transparent*. You can't see the eyes of the person wearing them.

GRAMMAR IN ACTION

3 Complete the conversation with *must*, *might*, and *can't* and phrases from the box.

be doing that	be right	be studying	be wrong	have basketball practice	know the answer

A What did you answer for question 10? I put 65.5.
B I put 75.3. We [1] ________________ both ________________. One of us [2] ________________.
A Why don't we ask Tim? He [3] ________________. He's good at math.
B Sure, but where is he?
A I'm not sure. He [4] ________________ in the library or he [5] ________________.
B No, he [6] ________________. Basketball practice is on Tuesday and today is Wednesday.
A OK, let's try to find him in the library then.

4 Match 1–5 with a–e. Complete the sentences with *have/has to*, *don't/doesn't have to*, *must/must not*, or *had to/didn't have to*.

1 Eric got up early yesterday because he ________________ ☐
2 This seat is reserved for older people, so you ________________ ☐
3 I have a lot to do tomorrow, so I really ________________ ☐
4 My friend had his car, so we ________________ ☐
5 Before visitors enter the exhibition, they ________________ ☐

a sit there.
b start work at 7 a.m.
c take the bus.
d put their bags in a locker.
e go to bed soon.

Self-Assessment

I can talk about senses.	☹	😐	☺
I can describe texture, sound, taste, etc.	☹	😐	☺
I can use modals of deduction and possibility.	☹	😐	☺
I can use modals of obligation, prohibition, necessity, and advice.	☹	😐	☺

LEARN TO ... PLAN YOUR HOMEWORK

When you have a lot of homework to do, it's important to decide what order to do it in and when to do it.

1 **Ask and answer questions 1–4 in the pamphlet with a partner. Are your answers similar or different?**

Feeling Stressed about Homework?

With our useful advice, you don't need to panic!

How often have you …

1 forgotten what you had to do for homework?
2 handed in a piece of homework late because you didn't start it on time?
3 started when you were too tired?
4 done the quick or easy homework first and then not had time for more difficult things?

If you answered "often" or "always," then you really need our help!

a Decide when you need to start your homework and give yourself enough time.
b When you ought to start but don't want to, tell yourself, "I'll just do five minutes." Once you start, it's easy to continue.
c You should think about how difficult a piece of homework is and how much time it needs.
d When you get your homework, write it down immediately and always in the same place.

Now use our homework planner and start planning!

2 **Match advice a–d with the problems in questions 1–4.**

1 ________ 2 ________ 3 ________ 4 ________

3 **Helen is planning her homework. What should she do first and last on Saturday? Why?**

Homework Planner Student's Name: Helen

1 What is the subject and homework task?	2 When do I have to hand the homework in?	3 From 1–5, how easy/difficult is it? 1= very easy, 5= very difficult	4 How much time do I need to do it?	5 What day am I going to do it?	6 On each day, what am I going to do first, second, etc.?
math, p38 exercises 6–9	Monday	3	45 minutes	Saturday	
history, essay	Monday	5	1 1/2 hours	Saturday	
science, p67 exercises 3 and 4	Monday	4	1 hour	Saturday	
geography, project	Wednesday	4	2 1/2 hours	Sunday	

SHAPE IT!

4 **Think about the homework you have to do this week. Use the homework planner to plan it.**

1 FINISHED?

1 **Put the letters in order to make words to describe clothes and shoes.**

1 

flowery

2 

______

3 

______

4 

______

5 

______

6 

______

7 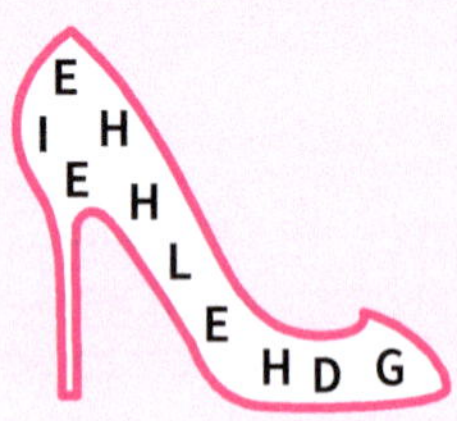

______

8 

______

2 **Match the texts with photos a–d.**

1 I've just had a totally amazing time! I've been looking at all kinds of interesting animals, with a lot of fantastic colors. I haven't done anything like this before, but I'd like to do it again. I've told all my friends, and they want to do it with me next time. ______

2 We've just come back, and we've spent all our money. The good news is now I have a lot of really good clothes, so I don't need to do anything like this again for a long time! ______

3 I've been outside all day, and now I'm feeling pretty tired. I've being doing this since I was very young, and one day I want to train other people to do the same as me. ______

4 I've had a pretty bad experience. I haven't tasted anything so bad in a long time. And since I had it, I've been feeling really sick. My stomach has been hurting for ages. I'm never going back there, and I'm going to tell all my friends about it! ______

a 

b 

c 

d 

3 **Complete the modifiers with vowels. Make sentences about you with the modifiers and the words in the box.**

amazed	better	confused	good at
happier	happy	more interesting	
shocked	slow	slower	taller

1 absolutely
2 _xtr_m_ly
3 r_ _lly
4 t_t_lly
5 f_ _rly
6 pr_tty
7 _ l_t
8 _ l_ttl_
9 _ b_t

4 **Put the letters in order to make verbs related to clothes and shoes.**

1 WIGOHT GO WITH
2 MTCAH ☐☐☐☐☐
3 TIF ☐☐☐
4 WERTAUO ☐☐☐☐ ☐☐☐
5 KOOLDOGONO ☐☐☐☐ ☐☐☐☐ ☐☐
6 HAPNUG ☐☐☐☐ ☐☐
7 LOFD ☐☐☐☐
8 PUPIZ ☐☐☐ ☐☐
9 NUZPI ☐☐☐☐☐

2 FINISHED?

1 **Read the clues and complete the crossword.**

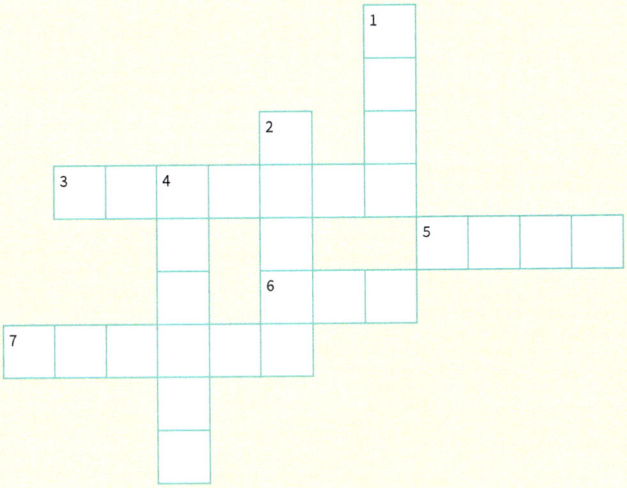

Across

3 I had to do … my phone for a week because it was broken.

5 Last week, I went … to my old elementary school to visit my teacher.

6 I feel bad. I hope I don't … up getting sick.

7 I've … up for piano lessons.

Down

1 I … through a difficult time when I started my new school, but now everything's OK.

2 Sara … out of her old apartment and went to live in a new one.

4 I … down three party invitations last month because I was so busy.

2 **Compare the pictures. How many sentences can you write about Stuart's life in the past with *used to*, *didn't use to*, and *would*? Use your imagination!**

When Stuart was a student, he used to live in an apartment.

____

____

3 **What movies had you seen by the time you were ten? Write as many as possible in two minutes.**

4 **Find words in the sentences that rhyme with parts of objects. Change them so the sentences make sense.**

1 Put the ~~kid~~ back or the pen will dry. lid

2 I've broken the sandal on my bag. ______

3 My computer needs a hug. ______

4 The Swiss play on that phone is really bright. ______

5 Don't get the camera pens dirty. ______

6 The map of my bag hurts my shoulder. It's too tight. ______

3 FINISHED?

1 Match the squares to make cooking verbs.

ro	ch	over	gri	sea	pe	sli	fr	ba	spre	gra	bo
y	son	te	ke	ll	il	ad	ast	cook	ce	el	op

2 Use the code to write the questions. Answer them so they are true for you.

A = ⚮	B = ☞	C = ■	D = ✘	E = ✈
F = ●	G = ❍	H = ✧	I = ❄	J = ✍
K = ✉	L = ✎	M = ✢	N = ✪	O = ✓
P = ☎	Q = ✾	R = ✇	S = ❏	T = ✐
U = ✳	V = ✶	W = ✂	X = ✆	Y = ✻

1 ✘✓❄✪❍ ✐✧❄❏ ✈✶✈✪❄✪❍
What are you ______________________________?
____

2 ❍✓❄✪❍ ✐✓ ✘✓ ✪✈✆✐ ❏✳✢✢✈✇
What are you ______________________________?
____

3 ☎✈✓☎✎✈ ✂❄✎✎ ✐✇⚮✶✈✎ ❄✪ ✐✧✈ ●✳✐✳✇✈
How do you think ______________________________?
____

4 ✂✈⚮✐✧✈✇ ❍✓❄✪❍ ✐✓ ☞✈ ✎❄✉✈ ✐✓✢✓✇✇✓✂
What's the ______________________________?
____

3 Make sentences with the future continuous or future perfect form of the verbs in the box.

chat with friends do homework
have dinner listen to music
play sports sleep

At 5 p.m. I will / won't be …
At 7 p.m. …
By midnight I will / won't have …

____
____
____
____
____
____
____

4 Circle nine more quantities.

H	A	N	D	F	U	L	T	G	F	D
V	Y	D	B	E	H	E	E	D	G	X
S	P	R	I	N	K	L	E	C	C	O
L	K	J	K	C	O	I	C	P	E	W
E	A	S	A	W	U	S	V	I	A	E
E	J	P	D	F	B	P	I	E	C	E
P	Q	O	F	V	B	L	L	C	H	J
O	I	O	V	C	K	A	W	E	U	K
P	J	N	E	D	A	S	G	O	N	R
C	H	F	C	W	Y	H	N	D	K	N
Q	R	U	J	H	Q	B	G	G	R	T
W	S	L	I	C	E	H	T	I	O	M

4 FINISHED?

1 Can you figure out these riddles?

1 Sometimes they look like faces; sometimes they look like animals. They're always changing shape. Gray ones usually disappear after the rain.

____

2 It looks like a tear and it tastes a bit like an apple. It sounds the same as two things of the same size that are used together.

____

3 Mine sounds like a bird. Mary's latest one sounds like a famous pop song. We don't know what Dave's sounds like because he always has his phone on silent.

____

2 Look at the photos. In your notebook, describe the things and guess what they might be.

1

2

3

4
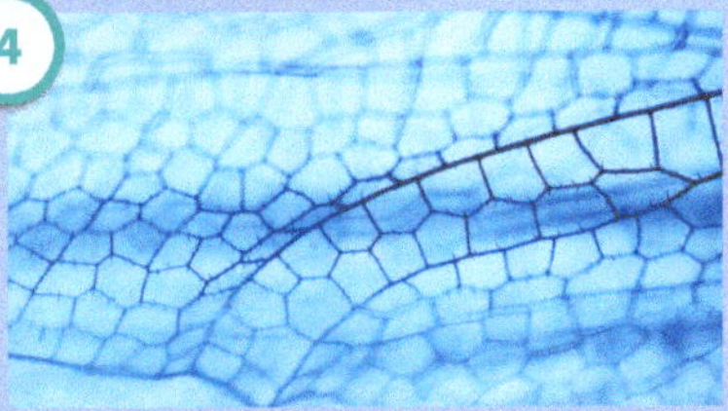

3 Imagine you do an unusual job. Write as many of these as possible in three minutes.

- things you had to do to get your job

- things you have to do every day in your job

Show your list to a partner. Can they guess the job?

4 Circle nine more adjectives.

R	U	Z	D	H	S	W	I	D	D	T	W
C	O	L	M	S	H	A	R	P	F	R	C
F	G	U	J	T	I	C	Y	L	S	A	O
N	A	X	G	H	N	A	B	U	M	V	L
B	V	I	D	H	Y	L	Q	S	E	U	O
S	K	L	N	D	E	F	E	B	L	H	R
P	M	P	R	T	K	M	U	Z	L	E	F
N	F	O	Z	G	S	P	I	C	Y	N	U
M	A	S	O	U	R	O	W	J	U	C	L
E	D	R	M	T	P	A	S	I	L	J	E
O	S	Q	U	G	H	T	V	Z	N	I	F
T	R	A	N	S	P	A	R	E	N	T	H

STARTER VOCABULARY BANK

Travel

accommodation

backpacking

resort

sightseeing

tourist attraction

trip

Music and Theater

audience	part	scene
lines	rehearsal	show

1 Are the sentences true or false?

1. An audience is all the actors in a play. ___
2. A resort is a store where you go to book a vacation. ___
3. The lines in a play are the words the actors speak. ___
4. Your accommodation is the plane, boat, etc., that takes you to your vacation. ___
5. Actors have rehearsals to practice their performance. ___

Ways of Communicating

describe	post	shout	translate	whisper
greet	shake hands	smile	wave	

2 Circle the correct words.

1. At the beginning of the trip, we were *posted* / *greeted* / *waved* by our tour guide.
2. I think he enjoyed the show because he was *shouting* / *waving* / *smiling*.
3. Alfonso will *describe* / *translate* / *whisper* all the tourist attractions we are going to see.
4. She plays the part of an angry teacher who *shouts* / *posts* / *smiles* at her students a lot.
5. In the first scene, two actors meet and *translate* / *shake hands* / *describe*.

LEARN TO LEARN

Personalizing Vocabulary

Writing personalized sentences helps you learn new words.

3 Choose four verbs from the list above and write sentences that are true for you. Then tell your partner.

1. ______________________________
2. ______________________________
3. ______________________________
4. ______________________________

Our teacher greets us every morning.

1 VOCABULARY BANK

Describing Clothes and Shoes

baggy

checkered

cotton

denim

flowery

high-heeled

leather

long-sleeved

plain

polka-dot

striped

tight

1 Is the adjective order correct or incorrect? Circle the correct answer.

1 We have to wear leather high-heeled shoes. *Correct / Incorrect*
2 Paul was wearing a red baggy T-shirt. *Correct / Incorrect*
3 Laura bought a flowery cotton blouse. *Correct / Incorrect*
4 I'd like a denim black jacket. *Correct / Incorrect*
5 The singer wore tight striped pants. *Correct / Incorrect*

Verbs Related to Clothes and Shoes

fit	go with	match	zip up
fold	hang up	unzip	
go out of style	look good on	wear out	

2 Circle the correct words.

1 I can't wear this polka-dot scarf. It doesn't *hang up / go with / fold* my coat.
2 This dress is a bit tight. It doesn't *match / unzip / fit* me any more.
3 I've had this sweater for years. It never seems to *wear out / look good on me / unzip me.*
4 Don't leave your jacket on the floor. *Hang it up / Do it up / Wear it out* in your closet.
5 You look great in that checkered shirt. It really *goes out of style / looks good on you / goes with you.*

LEARN TO LEARN

Categorizing

Recording new words in categories helps you remember their meaning.

3 Put the verbs related to clothes and shoes above in the correct categories. Compare with a partner.

Putting Clothes Away	
Ways of Saying That Clothes Look Good	fit
Reasons Not to Wear Clothes	
Putting On and Taking Off Clothes	

2 VOCABULARY BANK

Phrasal Verbs: Changes

do without	go back	look forward to	move to	sign up	turn down
end up	go through	move out	settle down	try out	turn out

1 **Complete the statements with a phrasal verb from the list. Then put them in order from most true for you (1) to least true for you (5). Compare with a partner.**

1 I would love to ______________ New York. ___
2 I never ______________ party invitations. ___
3 I always ______________ my English classes. ___
4 I like to ______________ new video games with my friends. ___
5 I would like to ______________ in one place for my whole life. ___

Parts of Objects

button

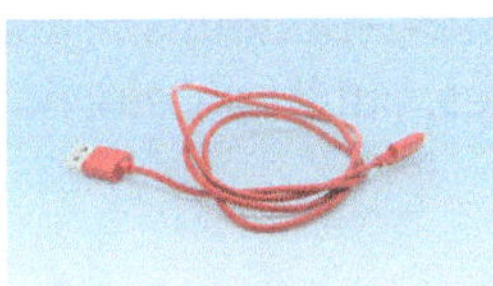
cord

cover

display

handle

key

lens

lid

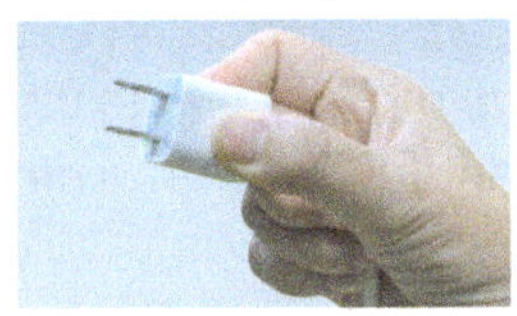
plug

strap

2 **Use the clues to complete the puzzle.**

1	l	e	n	s				I am made of glass. You look through me.
2								I am round. You press me to make an elevator come.
3								I am made of paper. I go on a book to protect it.
4								I am thin. You use me to fasten something.
5								I show information, for example, the time.

LEARN TO LEARN

Visualizing Words in Different Situations

Visualizing words in different situations helps you remember them.

3 **Where would you find these parts of objects (1–4)? Use the objects from the box. Some may have more than one part. Then choose two more parts from the list above and think of objects that have them.**

door jam jar keyboard laptop saucepan shoe box TV vacuum cleaner

1 key ______________
2 handle ______________
3 lid ______________
4 plug ______________

______________ ______________

3 VOCABULARY BANK

Cooking Verbs

bake

boil

chop

fry

grate

grill

overcook

peel

roast

season

slice

spread

1 Put the verbs in the correct place so that this potato recipe makes sense.

First, [1]*overcook* the potatoes and [2]*peel* them into large pieces. Add two spoonfuls of oil and [3]*roast* them with some salt and pepper. [4]*Chop* the potatoes in the oven for 45 minutes, but be careful not to [5]*season* them!

1 ________ 2 ________ 3 ________ 4 ________ 5 ________

Quantities

a bag of a chunk of	a cup of a handful of	a piece of a pinch of	a slice of a splash of	a spoonful of a sprinkle of

2 Match 1–5 with a–e.

1 This sauce isn't sweet enough. I'm going to add a spoonful of
2 I'm cooking tonight. We're having a lovely piece of
3 Grill the fish with a pinch of
4 I'm going to fry the potatoes with a splash of
5 The soup will be delicious because she's putting in a handful of

a sugar.
b oil.
c fresh herbs.
d beef.
e salt.

LEARN TO LEARN

Word Partners

When you learn new words, try to learn words that go with them so that you can use them in natural contexts.

3 Choose three quantities and think of four food items to go with each one. Compare with a partner.

4 VOCABULARY BANK

The Five Senses

feel feel like	look look like	smell smell like	sound sound like	taste taste like	touch

1 Complete the sentences with the words in the box.

a train delicious fresh bread icy stone

1 Has someone been baking? It smells like ________________ in here.
2 It's actually wood, but it's so cold, it feels like ________________.
3 I don't know what's in this dish, but it tastes ________________.
4 I heard a loud noise. It sounded a bit like ________________.
5 Be careful when you go outside. The pavement looks ________________.

Describing Texture, Sound, Taste, Etc.

colorful

faint

rough

sharp

shiny

smelly

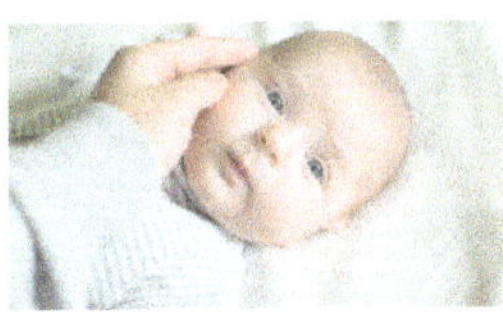
smooth

sour

spicy

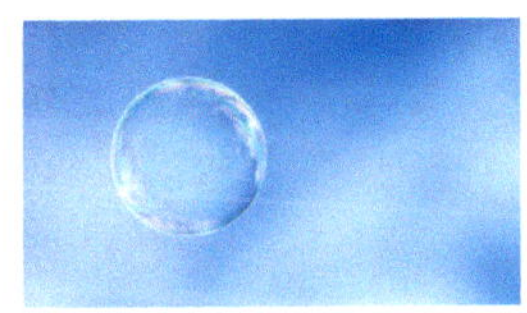
transparent

2 Match 1–5 with a–e.

1 You've worn that shirt for three days.
2 Be careful with that knife.
3 The noise can't be coming from this room.
4 Antonio washed his car yesterday.
5 I think it must be lemon juice.

a It tastes pretty sour.
b It's too faint.
c It must be a bit smelly.
d It looks very sharp.
e That's why it's so shiny.

LEARN TO LEARN

Using Your Senses

Using your senses can help you remember new words. Find objects that look, sound, taste, feel, or smell like the new words.

3 Choose three of the words from the list above and think of words connected to the senses.

shiny: shoes, hair, gold, metal, glass, car, clean

2 HISTORY

1 Look at the title and picture and discuss the questions.

1 When do you think this picture was taken?

2 Where are the people and what are they doing?

2.14 **2 Read the text. Check your answer to question 2 in Exercise 1.**

STARTING AGAIN

Between 1880 and 1910, 17 million Europeans made the decision to move to the United States and start a new life. Many of them never went back to their country of birth. This was part of what is known as the Great Atlantic **Migration**. It started in the 1840s and it is the largest migration in history.

For many people, it was the first time they had ever left their hometown. The two-week journey was very unpleasant, and on larger ships, up to 2,000 people were **crammed** into the lower **decks**. It was dark, there was little fresh water, and the air was **rancid**. So, why choose to go through such a difficult experience?

One major reason was hunger. For example, in Ireland in the 1840s, people used to depend on potatoes for food. When the potato crop failed for three years in a row, there was not enough to eat and around one million people died. After this, half of the Irish population decided to move to the United States. They were nervous about the journey, but they looked forward to a better life.

> I am exceedingly well pleased at coming to this land of plenty.

Letter from an Irish immigrant to The Times, *London, 1850*

Immigrants from all over Europe had their own story to tell. Although they had never experienced life in the United States before, they arrived ready to **settle** in a new culture. Immigrants helped build the United States into the country it is today. Like all migrations, the Great Atlantic Migration is the story of people making difficult decisions for the chance to start again.

3 Read the text again. Write *T* (true), *F* (false), or *DS* (doesn't say).

1 Most immigrants to the United States eventually returned to their country of birth. ___

2 There wasn't much room on board the ships. ___

3 Poverty was a major reason for migration. ___

4 Irish immigrants felt hopeful about their future. ___

5 Immigrants from all over Europe moved for the same reasons as the Irish. ___

6 Immigrants made a positive contribution to American society. ___

4 Discuss other possible causes of migration throughout history and up to the present day.

5 Complete the definitions with the words in bold in the text.

1 ____________ (n) the act of moving from one place to another

2 ____________ (n) the floors of a ship

3 ____________ (v) to make a home

4 ____________ (v) to be filled with something so there is no more room

5 ____________ (adj) having a very bad smell (or taste)

Explore It!

Guess the correct answer.

How many people live in a country different from the one they were born in?

a over 50 million

b over 150 million

c over 250 million

Find another interesting fact about migration. Write a question for your partner to answer.

4 SCIENCE

Echolocation

Imagine you are walking with a flashlight through a forest at night. Suddenly, the light goes out and you cannot see a thing. You feel a branch brush your face and smell the leaves on the trees. You need to go home, but how can you find your way?

If you were a bat, you would use echolocation. Echolocation is a technique used by some animals to move around in the dark. It helps them identify friends and enemies and "see" where they are going. Here are two examples of how animals use it.

Bats

To hunt for insects in the dark, bats make a **high-pitched** call as they fly, then listen for the returning **echo**. They calculate how far away something is by how long it takes the echo to return. A bat can **detect** an insect in the dark from a distance of five meters!

Dolphins

To identify objects in deep, dark waters, dolphins produce high-frequency **clicks**. These create sound waves that **bounce back** as echoes. This information helps dolphins figure out the distance, direction of travel, speed, and size of things.

But you don't have to be a bat or a dolphin to echolocate. You might be surprised to learn that some humans can echolocate, too. One such person is Daniel Kish. Daniel is completely blind, so he gets information about what is around him by clicking his tongue and listening to the echo. This technique allows him to safely ride a bike or go hiking in the wild. He also trains other blind people to echolocate. Amazing, isn't it?

1 Discuss the questions.

1 What special skills do the animals in the pictures have?

2 What do they use these skills for?

2 Read the article. Check your answers to Exercise 1. 4.10

3 Complete the chart with information from the article.

	Sound	How It Helps
Bat		
Dolphin		
Daniel Kish		

4 Complete the text with the words in bold from the article.

Whales, like dolphins, produce [1] ______________ to figure out an object's distance, direction, speed, and size. These sounds can be low- or [2] ______________. The sounds hit an object and [3] ______________ to the whale's throat. The time it takes the [4] ______________ of these sounds to return to the whale helps the animal [5] ______________, or sense, what is around it.

Explore It!

Guess the correct answer.

Some bats have a scream as loud as a …

a jet engine 30 meters away.

b very loud opera singer.

c machine that breaks rocks.

Find another interesting fact about bats, whales, or echolocation. Write a question for your partner to answer.

PRONUNCIATION

UNIT 1

The Letters *ea*

1.08 **1 Listen and repeat.**

1 /e/ br**ea**d 2 /iː/ m**ea**t 3 /eɪ/ st**ea**k

2 Put the words in the correct column according to the pronunciation of the letters ea.

~~break~~ clean great head jeans please

/e/	/iː/	/eɪ/
		break

1.09 **3 Listen, check, and repeat.**

UNIT 2

Used To

2.04 **1 Listen and repeat.**

1 He used to go out with his friends every weekend.
2 Did you use to like cats when you were younger?

2.05 **2 Listen to the sentences. Are the words in bold pronounced the same in each sentence?**

1 She **used a** friend's phone to call her parents.
2 She **used to** have her mom's phone.

2.06 **3 Listen and write the sentences.**

1 ______________________________
2 ______________________________
3 ______________________________
4 ______________________________

4 Practice saying the sentences.

1 She used to play basketball after school.
2 My dad used to listen to classical music.
3 Did you use to live here?

2.07 **5 Listen and check.**

UNIT 3

The Letters *ch*

3.03 **1 Listen and repeat.**

1 /ʃ/ ma**ch**ine 2 /tʃ/ **ch**eese 3 /k/ s**ch**ool

2 Put the words in the correct column according to the pronunciation of the letters *ch*.

~~chef~~ **ch**emistry **ch**op lun**ch** me**ch**anic musta**ch**e para**ch**ute stoma**ch**ache su**ch** whi**ch**

/ʃ/	/tʃ/	/k/
chef		

3.04 **3 Listen, check, and repeat.**

UNIT 4

Weak Form of *To*

4.06 **1 Listen and repeat.**

1 He has to work late tonight.
2 I need to buy new shoes.
3 We ought to take an umbrella.

4.07 **2 Listen and underline the stressed words.**

1 I'd <u>like</u> to <u>know</u> what <u>time</u> the <u>movie</u> <u>starts</u>.
2 We have to leave early tomorrow.
3 You ought to study more for your exams.
4 Do you need to make a phone call?

4.07 **3 Listen, check, and repeat.**

SHAPE IT! 4

COMBO A

WORKBOOK

Eoin Higgins and Philip Wood

CAMBRIDGE
UNIVERSITY PRESS

CONTENTS

STARTER

WELCOME!

VOCABULARY AND READING

Travel

1 ☆ **Match the words with the definitions.**

accommodation backpacking resort sightseeing tourist attractions ~~trip~~

1 a journey where you visit a place for a short time and then come back again trip

2 visiting places that are interesting because they are historical, famous, etc. ______

3 traveling or walking, carrying your things in a bag on your back ______

4 monuments or places that people on vacation like to visit ______

5 a town or place where people go on vacation, very often next to the ocean ______

6 a place where you live or stay ______

2 ☆ **Complete the sentences with information that is true for you. (See the *Learn to Learn* tip in the Student's Book, p4.)**

1 ______ is a famous tourist attraction in my country.

2 For our accommodation on our last vacation, we stayed in ______.

3 ______ is a popular resort in my country.

4 The last trip I went on was to ______.

5 In my opinion, going backpacking is a ______ way to spend your vacation.

6 I would like to go sightseeing in ______.

Music and Theater

3 ☆☆ **Complete the text. The first letter of each word is given.**

I was very surprised when Ms. Bayliss gave me the biggest [1]part ______ in the school musical. It wasn't easy to learn all my [2]l______, but after several [3]r______, I knew them perfectly. I was nervous on the day of the [4]s______ because my whole family was in the [5]a______. But everything went well, and after the final [6]s______, everyone stood up and clapped!

An Interview

4 ☆ **Read the interview. What did Jed do on vacation? Choose the correct photo.**

a 

b 

MIA So, where did you go on vacation, Jed?

JED Italy – it was a fantastic trip!

MIA Did you stay at a resort?

JED No, it was a hotel. We did a lot of sightseeing. We went to some famous tourist attractions, like the Colosseum in Rome. It was amazing!

MIA So, what was the best part of your trip?

JED Oh, that was when we saw an opera: *The Barber of Seville* in the Teatro Argentina – it's almost 300 years old! It's an amazing place – so beautiful!

MIA But wasn't the opera in Italian?

JED Yes, it was, and most of the audience was Italian, but there were subtitles.

5 ☆☆ **Read the interview again and answer the questions.**

1 Where did Jed stay?

______

2 What did Jed think of the Colosseum?

______

3 What else did Jed do in Rome?

______

4 Why could Jed understand the opera?

______

GRAMMAR IN ACTION AND VOCABULARY

Past and Present, Simple and Continuous

1 ★★ **Write the sentences in the past.**

1 Dan is reading the paper.
Dan was reading the paper.

2 They aren't listening to music.
____

3 Am I making a lot of noise?
____

4 Beth usually plays soccer on Saturdays.
____

5 They don't live in an apartment.
____

6 Does Michael like school?
____

2 ★★ **Complete the conversation with the verbs in the box in the correct tense.**

~~be~~ do enjoy have help visit

A How [1] ___*was*___ your trip to Paris?

B Great, thanks! I [2] __________ it a lot!

A What [3] __________ you __________ there?

B We [4] __________ a lot of tourist attractions!

A You're so lucky! While you [5] __________ a great time in Paris, I [6] __________ my dad paint the house!

3 ★★★ **Answer the questions with information that is true for you.**

1 What did you do last weekend?
____

2 What were you doing at nine o'clock last night?
____

3 What does your dad do?
____

4 What's your mom probably doing at the moment?
____

Ways of Communicating

4 ★ **Circle eight more communication verbs in the word snake.**

postshoutwhisperdescribesmiletranslateshakehandsgreetwave

5 ★★ **Complete the chart with the verbs from Exercise 4. Some verbs go in both columns.**

You Can Use Your Hands to Do This	You Can Use Your Mouth to Do This
1 *post*	6 ______
2 ______	7 ______
3 ______	8 ______
4 ______	9 ______
5 ______	10 ______
	11 ______

6 ★★ **Complete the sentences with the verbs from Exercise 4.**

1 Do you know anyone who can ___*translate*___ from English into Chinese?

2 Did you __________ a comment on my blog?

3 Please don't __________! I can hear you!

4 How would you __________ your personality?

5 When you __________, you feel happier.

6 If you don't know the answer when the teacher asks you, I'll __________ it to you very quietly.

7 When movie stars arrive at the Oscars, they often __________ to the crowd.

8 When I have my interview tomorrow, how should I __________ the person who is interviewing me? Should I __________ with them?

LISTENING AND GRAMMAR IN ACTION

A Conversation

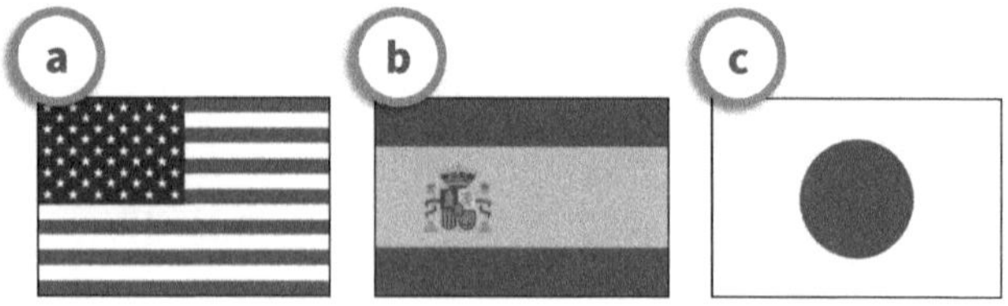

1 ☆☆ **Match the flags a–c with the countries 1–3.**

1 Spain ___ 2 Japan ___ 3 the U.S.A. ___

🎧 S.01 2 ☆ **Listen to the conversation. Which of the countries from Exercise 1 does the girl's dad sometimes go to?**

____

🎧 S.01 3 ☆☆ **Listen again. Put the pictures a–f in the order that they are mentioned.**

4 ☆☆☆ **Answer the questions.**

1 Which country would you like to visit? Why?

____

2 Would you like to travel a lot for your job? Why?

____

3 Do you think people smile a lot in your country? Give a reason for your answer.

____

Present Perfect and Simple Past

5 ☆ **Complete the sentences with the words in the box. There are two extra words.**

at ever for from ~~have~~ never 's since

1 ___*Have*___ you finished the book?
2 We've been here ___________ four o'clock.
3 Have you ___________ been to Japan?
4 John's studied French ___________ three years.
5 I've ___________ seen snow before.
6 Beth ___________ sent me a message.

6 ☆☆ **(Circle) the correct options.**

1 Last year, I (*went*) / *'ve been* to London.
2 *Did you ever climb / Have you ever climbed* a mountain?
3 My sister *liked / 's liked* chocolate since she was a baby.
4 I *didn't do / haven't done* my homework. I'm going to start now!
5 I *called / 've called* you just a minute ago!
6 We *were / 've been* at the mall for three hours now!

7 ☆☆ **Complete the text with the simple past or present perfect form of the verb in parentheses.**

TO: Aidan

FROM: Paola

Hi Aidan,

I [1] *'ve been* (be) in Rome for almost a week now. I [2] ___________ (arrive) last Friday. My Italian [3] ___________ (not get) much better, which isn't very surprising, really. I need more time. I [4] ___________ (do) a lot of sightseeing! Yesterday I [5] ___________ (go) to the Vatican. The museum is incredible! I [6] ___________ (eat) some very good food because the woman I'm staying with is a great cook. Last night she [7] ___________ (make) *cannelloni al ragù*. Tomorrow, I start at the language school. I [8] ___________ (not feel) so happy or excited for a long time!

Love, Paola

WRITING

An Informal Email

1 **Read Jack's email to his friend Ethan. Which two of the activities in the pictures a–c did he do?**

a 

b 

c 

TO: Ethan@postit.com

FROM: Jack@comunica.com

SUBJECT: News!

[1]Hi Ethan,

1 [2]How are things? Are you enjoying life in Mexico? [3]I just wanted to get in contact because I haven't sent you an email for a long time. Sorry about that!

2 I've been really busy lately. I'm in the school play, and we've had a lot of rehearsals after school. I have a big part, so it hasn't been easy to learn all my lines! But I think I've finally managed to do it. I hope so because the play's next week! Have you ever done any acting? Perhaps you can give me some advice!

3 Last Saturday was my dad's 50th birthday, so he took us all out for a meal in a really nice restaurant in the country. All his brothers and sisters came, and everyone gave him a present. I gave him a D.C. United soccer scarf because he's a big fan. I think he liked it!

4 So, that's my news. When are you coming back to visit?

[4]Bye for now!

[5]Take care,

Jack

2 **Read the email again. Match the paragraphs (1–4) with the information (A–D).**

A say goodbye ☐
B things Jack has done recently ☐
C things Jack did at a particular time ☐
D say hello and why you're writing ☐

3 **Look at paragraphs 2 and 3 again. What tenses does Jack use to describe his actions? Why?**

______
______
______

4 **Match the underlined phrases in the email 1–5 with the phrases a–e.**

a Love, ☐
b I'm writing to ☐
c Hello ☐
d See you soon! ☐
e How are you? ☐

PLAN

5 **Write an email to a friend in the U.S.A., telling them what you've done recently. Make two lists.**

1 Things I've done when the exact time is not important or that are not finished (present perfect):

______
______
______
______

2 Things I did at a particular time (simple past):

______
______
______
______

WRITE

6 **Write your email. Remember to include four paragraphs, your ideas from Exercise 5, vocabulary from this unit, and phrases from the *Useful Language* box (see Student's Book, p9).**

CHECK

7 **Do you ...**

- start and end the email correctly?
- give the reason why you are writing?
- use verbs in the correct tense?

1 What is fashion?

VOCABULARY

Describing Clothes and Shoes

1 ☆ Circle the correct adjectives to describe the clothes.

1 
a *cotton* / *denim* skirt

2 
a *tight* / *baggy* sweater

3 
a *plain* / *checkered* shirt

4 
baggy / *high-heeled* boots

5 
a *striped* / *flowery* T-shirt

6 
a *long-sleeved* / *polka-dot* dress

2 ☆☆ Complete the conversations with the words in the box. There are two extra words.

cotton	checkered	denim	flowery
high-heeled	leather	long-sleeved	~~tight~~

1 A Are those shorts OK?
  B No, I need a bigger size. They're very tight!

2 A Do you want a plain or a checkered T-shirt?
  B No, I want something really different! That ________ one is nice!

3 A What do you usually wear in the summer?
  B Cool clothes made of ________!

4 A Do you like my new black and white ________ shirt?
  B Not really! It looks like a chess board!

5 A Are you going to pack some jeans for your trip to Córdoba?
  B Are you joking? It's 40°C there at the moment! I don't want to wear anything made of ________!

6 A How often do you wear ________ shoes?
  B Not often. Only when I go to a party or formal dinner.

3 ☆ Match the adjectives 1–5 with the categories a–c. (See the *Learn to Learn* tip in the Student's Book, p11.)

1 baggy, tight — c
2 checkered, striped
3 denim, cotton
4 high-heeled, long-sleeved
5 plain, polka-dot

a material
b pattern
c shape

4 ☆☆ Put the words in the correct order.

1 a / checkered / red and green / shirt
  a red and green checkered shirt
2 a / skirt / denim / plain
  ____
3 jeans / cotton / tight / white
  ____
4 jacket / denim / red / baggy / a
  ____
5 striped / brown and blue / T-shirt / a / tight / cotton
  ____
6 brown and white / shoes / leather / polka-dot / high-heeled
  ____

5 ☆☆☆ Write four sentences about clothes that you like and don't like to wear. Use adjectives from Exercise 1.

____
____
____
____

Explore It!

Guess the correct answer.

In what decade did miniskirts become popular?

a the 1950s b the 1960s c the 1970s

Find another interesting fact about popular fashion in a past decade. Write a question and send it to a classmate in an email, or ask them in the next class.

READING

A Blog Entry

1 ☆ **Look at the text quickly and circle the correct answers.**

1 The text is a *an advertisement / a personal opinion.*

2 It's about *how often to wash jeans / what jeans to buy.*

2 ☆☆ **Read the blog entry. Check the meaning of the words in the box in a dictionary. Then complete the sentences.**

brand	claim	~~eliminate~~	harm	research	turn out

1 Cheese gives me a headache. I need to eliminate it from my diet.

2 Don't wash that shirt in very hot water. It will definitely ________ the material!

3 I'm going to do some ________ before I buy a new phone.

4 I like these jeans, but I don't know this ________. Is it any good?

5 Some people ________ that shopping online is 100 percent safe, but I'm not so sure.

6 I'm making a dress, but I have a feeling that it's not going to ________ well.

3 ☆☆ **Are the sentences *T* (true) or *F* (false)? Correct the false sentences.**

1 In the writer's opinion, the question of how often to wash jeans is very important.
F It's not the most important topic in the world.

2 The writer agrees with her friend about how often to wash jeans.
____

3 In the writer's opinion, an important person in the clothing industry has a strange idea.
____

4 Freezing jeans is a good way to clean them.
____

5 It's best not to wash your jeans too often.
____

6 The experts make a good recommendation.
____

4 ☆☆☆ **Do you think the information in the blog entry is useful and interesting? Why / Why not?**

____

____

____

NEW YORK CALLING! | **BLOG** | ABOUT ME | CONTACT ME

TO WASH OR NOT TO WASH JEANS? THAT IS THE QUESTION!

I haven't written an entry recently because I've been taking exams all week! Did you miss me? Today, I want to talk about a very important subject: how often to wash denim jeans! OK, maybe it's not the most important topic in the world, but people have very different ideas about it. One of my friends even thinks that you should never wash jeans because it harms them. I don't know about that! Imagine wearing a pair of tight jeans that you haven't washed for over a year! So, anyway, I decided to do some research online about how often you should actually wash jeans. One thing I read really surprised me: the head of a company that makes a very well-known brand of jeans says that he hardly ever washes his. He just puts them in the freezer. He claims that this keeps them clean! Speaking personally, I wouldn't want to put my jeans next to a bag of frozen peas! And it turns out that the "freezer theory" isn't correct. After you wear your jeans just once, they're covered in bacteria, skin cells, and the natural oils from your body. And freezing them won't eliminate these things. According to the experts, there is one good reason for not washing your jeans very often: they get a little baggier every time you wash them. And most of us don't want to wear baggy jeans! Experts actually say there's no specific recommended frequency for washing jeans – but you should definitely wash them when they start to smell! That sounds like good advice to me!

GRAMMAR IN ACTION

Present Perfect Simple and Present Perfect Continuous

1 ★★ Match the beginnings of the sentences 1–6 with the ends a–f.

1 I've done [b]
2 Jack's been playing soccer [ ]
3 Have they had [ ]
4 You've been wearing [ ]
5 Bethany hasn't been going [ ]
6 Has your dad finished cleaning [ ]

a that shirt all week!
b all my homework.
c the bathroom?
d for three hours!
e lunch yet?
f to the gym recently.

2 ★★ Complete the sentences with the verbs in parentheses. Use the present perfect simple (PPS) or present perfect continuous (PPC).

1 We _haven't made_ (not make) lunch yet. (PPS)
2 I ______ (do) a lot of clothes shopping recently. (PPC)
3 Ana ______ (visit) her family. (PPC)
4 ______ (they / finish) the game? (PPS)
5 My tablet ______ (not work) all day. (PPC)
6 My aunt ______ (have) a lot of different jobs. (PPS)

3 ★★ Circle the correct options.

1 I've *felt* / *(been feeling)* very tired recently.
2 John hasn't *answered* / *been answering* my last email.
3 Rachel isn't here. Has she *gone* / *been going* shopping?
4 Our neighbors have *made* / *been making* a lot of noise.
5 Why have *you bought* / *you been buying* three baggy sweaters?
6 *Did you study* / *Have you been studying* for your exams all week?

4 ★★ Write sentences in the present perfect simple or continuous.

1 what / you / do / recently?
What have you been doing recently?
2 I / finish / finally / my school project!
______
3 Nick / wear / the same clothes / all week.
______
4 you / ever / be / to Los Angeles?
______
5 I / try / to contact you / all day!
______
6 Jan / not decide / what to do
______

5 ★★★ Complete the messages with the correct form of the verbs in the box.

find	go shopping	~~look for~~	not buy	try on	wait

You [1] _'ve been looking for_ a dress for the party for a long time! [2] ______ you ______ anything yet? Maxine

No! And I [3] ______ for hours! I [4] ______ six different dresses, but I [5] ______ anything yet! Sarah

Well, I [6] ______ for you in the café for too long! I'm leaving! Maxine

6 ★★★ Write a sentence about something that you have or haven't done before and a sentence about something that you have or haven't been doing recently.

I've never been to Seattle.
I've been playing a lot of video games recently.
______
______
______
______

VOCABULARY AND LISTENING

Verbs Related to Clothes and Shoes

1 ☆ **Circle the correct options.**

1 These pants are very tight. They don't (fit) / *look good on* me.
2 Can you please *hang* / *fit* up the pants over there?
3 Could you help me *unzip* / *fold* my dress. I want to take it off.
4 People will still wear jeans in 100 years. They will never *wear out* / *go out of style*.
5 Do these shoes *go with* / *wear out* this dress?
6 You look great with those earrings. They really *match* / *look good on* you!

2 ☆☆ **Complete the text with words and phrases from Exercise 1.**

HOW TO LOOK GOOD!

- Some clothes [1] *go out of style* quickly! So, don't wear something that was popular last year!
- Your clothes must [2] ______ you perfectly! Don't buy something that you really like if it isn't the right size!
- Buy clothes with "easy" colors that [3] ______ a lot of other colors.
- Know what kinds of clothes [4] ______ you! Some people look great in stripes – but do you?
- Don't [5] ______ your clothes and put them in drawers. It's much better if you [6] ______ them ______.

3 ☆☆☆ **Write sentences that are true for you. (See the *Learn to Learn* tip in the Student's Book, p14.)**

1 How quickly do you wear out your clothes?

______

2 Do all your clothes fit you well? Give details.

______

3 What colors look good on you? Why?

______

4 Do you ever wear clothes that have gone out of style? Why / Why not?

______

An Interview

1.01 **4** ☆ **Listen to Caitlin talking about her job as a salesperson. Put the things she talks about in the correct order.**

a ☐ the bad points of the job
b ☐ the good points of the job
c ☐ why she wanted to work as a salesperson

1.01 **5** ☆☆ **Listen again and circle the correct options.**

1 Why did Caitlin decide to work as a salesperson in a clothing store?
   a She wants to work as a fashion designer.
   (b) She's very interested in clothes.
   c She likes helping people.
2 What are Caitlin's coworkers like?
   a They're nice.
   b Some are nice; some aren't.
   c She really likes her boss.
3 What happens every one or two months?
   a She buys clothes at a discount.
   b She helps with window displays.
   c New clothes arrive at the store.
4 How much of a discount does Caitlin get?
   a 15 percent
   b 50 percent
   c It depends on the clothes.
5 What are two negative aspects of the job?
   a Some of the jobs are a bit boring, and the pay isn't very good.
   b Some of the customers can be rude, and you're standing up all the time.
   c Some customers aren't polite, and not all the jobs are interesting.

GRAMMAR IN ACTION

Modifiers

1 ☆ **Read the phrases and circle the options that have the same meaning.**

1 absolutely wrong
  (a) totally wrong b a bit wrong
2 fairly nice
  a extremely nice b pretty nice
3 a lot more difficult
  a a bit more difficult b far more difficult
4 a bit bigger
  a a little bigger b far bigger
5 extremely tired
  a pretty tired b really tired
6 pretty far
  a fairly far b extremely far

2 ☆☆ **Look at the information from a price comparison website. Are the sentences *T* (true) or *F* (false)?**

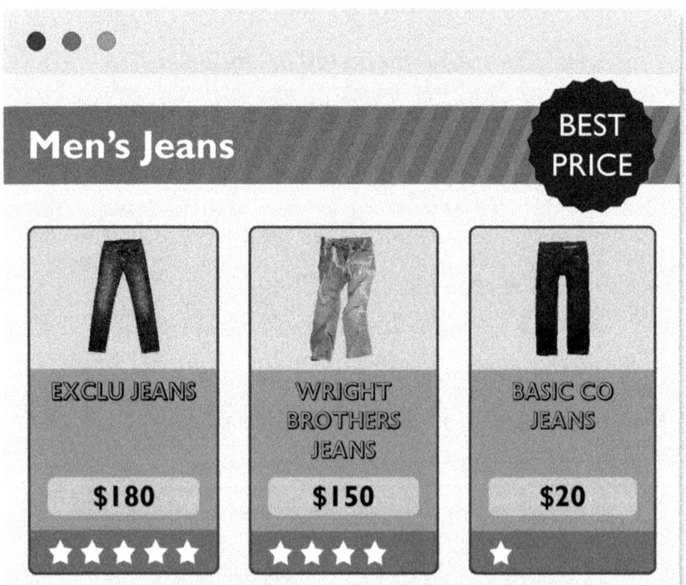

1 Exclu jeans are extremely expensive. T
2 Exclu jeans are far more expensive than Basic Co jeans. ___
3 Basic Co jeans aren't really cheap. ___
4 Wright Brothers jeans are a bit less expensive than Exclu jeans. ___
5 Basic Co jeans are pretty expensive. ___

3 ☆☆ **Circle the correct options.**

1 These pants aren't "a little" baggy. They're *pretty* / *extremely* baggy! (*extremely* circled)
2 Your watch was a bit more expensive than mine, but it's *a little* / *far* better! It's fantastic!
3 I'm *pretty* / *really* hungry, but I'm not very hungry.
4 The weather was *a bit* / *far* hotter than we imagined. It was a big surprise.
5 Mike's *fairly* / *really* generous. I think he's the most generous person I know.
6 I'm *fairly* / *totally* sure that the store's closed today, but maybe I'm wrong.

4 ☆☆ **Complete the conversation with the missing words. Circle the correct options.**

A How was your vacation in San Sebastian?
B Only [1] ______ good, I'm afraid.
A So, not [2] ______ fantastic?
B No. The weather was [3] ______ terrible. It rained all the time!
A Oh, no! What about the food? I've heard it's fantastic there – [4] ______ better than the food in the U.S.A.!
B Yes, it was [5] ______ delicious! I think it was [6] ______ more expensive than the U.S.A., but my dad said the prices weren't too bad.

1 a totally (b) fairly c far
2 a a lot b fairly c absolutely
3 a really b a bit c a little
4 a pretty b far c a little
5 a absolutely b pretty c a lot
6 a far b really c a bit

5 ☆☆☆ **Complete the sentences so they are true for you. Use modifiers from this page.**

1 Living in my hometown is ______________________.
2 My family is ______________________.
3 For me, buying clothes is ______________________.
4 When I compare English and math, I think English is ______________________.
5 In my opinion, soccer is ______________________.
6 When I compare drinking water or soda, I think ______________________.

WRITING

A Blog Comment

FIVE WAYS TO SPEND LESS MONEY ON CLOTHES

- Go to secondhand stores!
- Buy your clothes online!
- Swap clothes with friends!
- Only buy clothes on sale!
- Buy clothes with neutral colors (black, gray, or white). They'll go well with all your other clothes!

<u>Great post! Thanks for sharing!</u> TBH, I've always thought that buying clothes online was a bit dangerous. I mean, what happens if you get something and it doesn't fit you? That's a problem! But <u>since reading your post</u>, I've looked at some online clothing sites, and they really help you find the right size. What's more, some of the clothes are extremely inexpensive, especially if you buy from China or Hong Kong! I've just bought a flowery dress online, and it fits me perfectly! It's absolutely amazing! Sonya

Your post <u>really got me thinking about</u> how to save money on clothes! I've been spending too much recently, so it's become a BIG problem! IMO, going to secondhand stores is a really good idea. <u>I had no idea that</u> they had such great stuff! I thought they only had clothes that were out of style! I've already bought a great denim shirt and a cool polka-dot T-shirt. And <u>I've decided</u> to get all my clothes from secondhand stores in the future! They're far cheaper! Aidan

1 ★★ **Read the blog entry and the comments and answer the questions.**

1 What is the blog entry about?

____

2 Which ideas from the blog have Sonya and Aidan used?

____

2 ★★ **Read the comments again and answer the questions in your notebook.**

1 What do *TBH* and *IMO* mean?

2 Why does Sonya use an exclamation point in: *It's absolutely amazing!* ?

3 Why does Aidan use capital letters in: *It's become a BIG problem!* ?

3 ★★ **Complete the *Useful Language* phrases. Look at the <u>underlined</u> phrases in the blog for help.**

1 You really *got* me thinking about how much I spend.

2 I've been thinking and I've __________ to go shopping far less often.

3 Great __________! Thanks for __________!

4 I had __________ that buying online was so easy!

5 __________ reading your post, I've really started to think about how I shop.

PLAN

4 ★★ **Write your own blog comment. Choose one of the five ideas from the blog entry and take notes about these things.**

Do you like the idea? Why / Why not? ______________________________

____

Other ideas you would like to try in the future:

____

WRITE

5 ★★★ **Write your comment. Remember to include the present perfect simple and continuous, modifiers, vocabulary from this unit, phrases from the *Useful Language* box (see Student's Book, p.17), and the features from Exercise 2.**

CHECK

6 **Do you …**

- explain why an idea might or might not work well?
- explain what you would like to try in the future?

1 REVIEW

VOCABULARY

1 Complete the crossword. Use the clues.

ACROSS →

2 ________ pants
3 ________ shirt
6 ________ scarf
7 ________-________ dress
9 ________ sweater
10 ________ jeans
11 ________ skirt

2
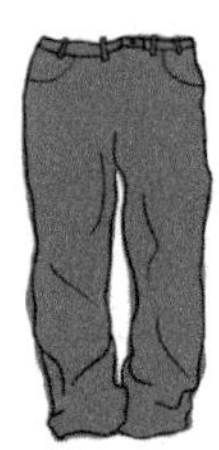

3

6

7
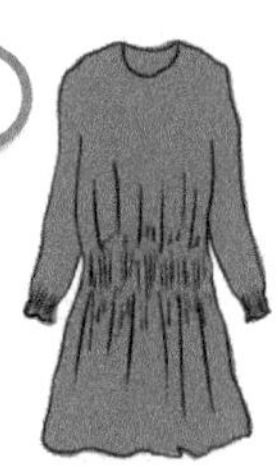

9

10

11

DOWN ↓

1 ________-________ shoes
4 ________-________ top
5 ________ skirt
6 ________ T-shirt
8 ________ shoes

1

4

5

6

8

2 Complete the sentences with the words in the box.

fit fold go out of style go with hang up look good on match unzip wear out zip up

1 I don't think these shoes will ________ soon. Sneakers are always popular.
2 You need to ________ your coat. It's very cold!
3 These shorts don't ________ me now, but they weren't too small last year!
4 Do you think these earrings ________ the color of my eyes?
5 I never wear brown. It doesn't ________ me.
6 I only ________ shirts when I pack a bag. I always ________ them ________ at home.
7 That shirt doesn't ________ those pants. They look terrible together!
8 You can ________ the zipper on the tent. It isn't raining anymore.
9 Those are nice shoes, so please don't play soccer in them. You'll ________ them ________ very quickly!

GRAMMAR IN ACTION

3 Complete the sentences with the present perfect simple or continuous form of the verbs in parentheses.

1 I ______________ (not see) that movie. Is it good?

2 Claudia ______________ (try) to buy tickets all afternoon!

3 Oh, no! I ______________ (lose) my earring!

4 Dan ______________ (never / play) chess.

5 I ______________ (finish)! I'm sorry you ______________ (wait) so long.

6 ______________ (we / buy) everything we need?

4 Read the conversations and circle the correct options.

1 **A** How was the party?
  B It was *really / pretty* good, but not amazing.

2 **A** Did you enjoy the movie!
  B Yes, it was *fairly / absolutely* amazing!

3 **A** How are you feeling?
  B Only *a little / a lot* better.

4 **A** Did you do well on your exams?
  B My results were *extremely / pretty* good, but they weren't fantastic.

5 **A** This school project is hard!
  B Yes, it is! It's *fairly / far* harder than Ms. Taylor said!

6 **A** I'm the best player on the team!
  B I'm sorry, but you're *fairly / totally* wrong about that!

CUMULATIVE LANGUAGE

5 Complete the email with the missing words. Circle the correct options.

TO: Amy   FROM: Zoe

Hi Amy,

How are you? I'm sorry that I [1] ______ for a while. I have a lot of news! I [2] ______ a course in fashion design, and it [3] ______ really well! I [4] ______ on a dress with a flowery design all week. I [5] ______ it because it's [6] ______ hard work. But I love it!

I [7] ______ that I want to work as a fashion designer in the future. I think it would be a [8] ______ awesome job – and [9] ______ more interesting than working in an office! How about you? [10] ______ life in Chile? Your Spanish must be [11] ______ fantastic now because it was [12] ______ good before!

Anyway, talk to you soon!

Zoe

	a	b	c
1	haven't written	haven't been writing	don't write
2	've been starting	start	've started
3	's gone	goes	's been going
4	work	've been working	've worked
5	haven't finished	don't finish	haven't been finishing
6	far	a little	really
7	decide	've decided	've been deciding
8	fairly	far	totally
9	far	pretty	a bit
10	Do you enjoy	Have you been enjoying	Have you enjoyed
11	a bit	a lot	absolutely
12	pretty	well	a lot

2 What can you change?

VOCABULARY
Phrasal Verbs: Changes

1 ★★ Circle the correct options.

1 Max has settled (down) / *up* well at his new school.
2 I'm really *looking* / *seeing* forward to next weekend.
3 I'm going to sign *up* / *down* for yoga classes.
4 Let's *try* / *do* out the new skate park.
5 I'm *having* / *going* through a hard time at the moment.
6 Are you going to turn *up* / *down* Juan's invitation?

2 ★★ Complete the sentences with the phrasal verbs in the box.

do without	end up	go back
move out	~~sign up~~	turn out

1 Did you ___sign up___ for the school trip to San Diego?
2 The party didn't ______________ very well in the end. Not many people came.
3 My sister wants to ______________ and be more independent.
4 If you don't work hard at school, you probably won't ______________ with a good job.
5 I don't think I could ______________ chocolate! I love it!
6 I probably won't ______________ to my hometown when I finish college.

3 ★★★ Complete the personality quiz with the correct form of the verbs in the box and the correct prepositions.

do go look forward ~~move~~ move sign try turn

Are You a Positive Person?

1 Would you like to ___move out___ of your family's home before you're 25?
2 In your life, do things usually ______________ well?
3 When you are ______________ a hard time, do you look for solutions?
4 Do you ______________ for a lot of optional activities at school?
5 Do you like to ______________ new ways of doing things?
6 When you get up, do you always ______________ everything you will do in the day?
7 Would you like to ______________ a new country?
8 Could you ______________ the Internet for a week?

4 ★ Answer *Yes* or *No* to the questions from Exercise 3. How positive are you?

7–8 *yes* answers: very positive!

5–6 *yes* answers: fairly positive!

Less than 5 *yes* answers: not very positive!

5 ★★★ Write four sentences with phrasal verbs about what kind of person you are. (See the *Learn to Learn* tip in the Student's Book, p23.)

____

____

____

____

Explore It!

Guess the correct answer.

What is the minimum age when you can start working in the U.S.A. without your parents' permission?

a 14 b 16 c 18

Find an interesting fact about when you can legally do something for the first time in your country. Write a question and send it to a classmate in an email, or ask them in the next class.

READING

A Blog Entry

1 ☆ **Look at the blog entry quickly. Why is Chloe's life new? Mark (✓) the correct answer.**

a She's just gotten married. ☐
b She's in college now. ☐
c She's just finished college. ☐

2 ☆☆ **Read the blog entry and check the meaning of the words in the box in a dictionary. Then complete the sentences.**

~~disappointed~~ into law lecture plenty of surrounded

1 I did badly on my exams. I'm really *disappointed* !
2 I'm really ______ comic books. They're my favorite thing to read.
3 The campsite was ______ by trees, so it was very beautiful.
4 My cousin's studying ______ . He says it's a lot of work.
5 I know ______ people, but do I have any real friends?
6 I've just been to a really interesting ______ .

3 ☆☆ **Read the first paragraph of the blog entry and answer the questions. Write "no information" if there is no answer in the text.**

1 Which college does Chloe go to?

______

2 What does Chloe mean when she says that you "have to start from zero"?

______

3 Why are things turning out well?

______

4 ☆☆ **Read the second paragraph of the blog entry and complete the chart.**

	Studying in High School	Studying in College
1	*classes in small groups*	
2		
3		

5 ☆☆☆ **Do you think it's a good idea to study away from home? Write three or four sentences.**

______
______
______
______
______

CHLOE'S CORNER BLOG ABOUT FAQS

A NEW LIFE!

Have you ever had a really special time in your life? Well, I'm having one now because I've just started college! I was really looking forward to it, and so far, I haven't been disappointed! My biggest worry before coming was: would it be easy to make new friends? It's a good question because when you go to college, you have to start from zero. The old friends you used to see at home aren't there anymore, so you need to create a completely new social life. Well, I'm glad to say that things are turning out really well. I'm living in a dorm, which is a special building just for students. It's the ideal place to be during your first year because you're surrounded by new faces! And everyone's into making new friends.

Studying in college feels very different from how things used to be in high school. Although there were a lot of students in my high school, there are over 100 students in my lectures now! In high school, we would have the chance to ask questions and discuss things with our teachers. Now you just sit down and take notes! Another big difference is that I only have 12 hours of lectures per week (I'm studying law). The rest of the time I spend studying alone. That can be pretty difficult because you need a lot of discipline! And there are plenty of other, more interesting things to do!

I've settled down really well into college life. There's just one "small" problem: I need to study more!

GRAMMAR IN ACTION

Used To, *Would*, and Simple Past

1 ☆☆ **Complete the sentences with the correct form of *used to* and the verbs in parentheses.**

1 I ___used to hate___ (hate) going to the dentist.
2 My dad ______________ (have) more hair.
3 I ______________ (not like) carrots.
4 My mom ______________ (not go) to the gym.
5 ______________ (you / play) the violin?
6 ______________ (Matt / be) your best friend?

2 ☆☆ **Rewrite the sentences with *used to* when it is possible.**

1 I went to bed at ten o'clock last night.
   not possible
2 In the past, did your grandpa ride a bike to work?
   ____
3 People went to the movies more often before the Internet.
   ____
4 Clothes didn't wear out so quickly before.
   ____
5 Oh, no! Did you leave the keys at home?
   ____
6 Was there a castle in this town before?
   ____

3 ☆☆☆ **Write four sentences about what people *used to* and *didn't use to* do. Use the photos for ideas.**

1 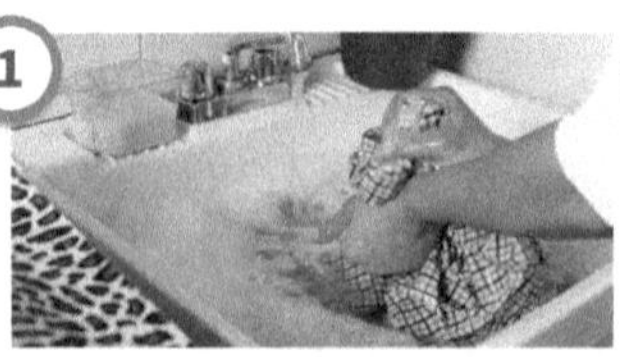

2 

3 

4 

1 ______________
2 ______________
3 ______________
4 ______________

4 ☆ **Circle the correct options.**

Things Were Different When I Was Young!

Children [1]*would* / *wouldn't* listen to their parents and teachers. Now they don't listen!

People [2]*would* / *wouldn't* run everywhere. They had more time.

We [3]*would* / *wouldn't* play in the street. It wasn't dangerous then.

People [4]*would* / *wouldn't* think about money all the time. They had better values.

Families [5]*would* / *wouldn't* go to another country on vacation. And some families didn't go anywhere!

We [6]*would* / *wouldn't* listen to the radio more because not everyone had a TV.

5 ☆☆ **Rewrite the underlined part of the sentences with *would*. If it isn't possible, rewrite the sentences with *used to*.**

1 We lived in the country before.
   We used to live in the country.
2 I often arrived late to school when I was younger.
   ____
3 Did you wear glasses before?
   ____
4 My grandma always went for a walk after breakfast.
   ____
5 My dad often swam in the ocean when he lived in Salvador.
   ____
6 My mom was a nurse before.
   ____

6 ☆☆ **Circle the correct option OR options.**

A [1]*Did you take* / *Did you use to take* tennis lessons?
B Yes, I did.
A So, why [2]*did* / *would* you stop?
B My teacher [3]*would* / *used to* criticize me all the time. So one day I [4]*decided* / *used to decide*, "No more tennis lessons!"
A Really? I [5]*didn't* / *didn't use to* know anything about that! Who [6]*did you* / *did you use to* take lessons with?
B My dad!

VOCABULARY AND LISTENING

Parts of Objects

1 ☆ **Find nine more parts of objects in the word search.**

B	O	L	S	L	E	N	S
H	B	U	T	T	O	N	D
A	C	O	R	D	O	W	P
N	R	C	A	B	O	E	L
D	I	M	P	Z	A	Y	U
L	L	C	O	V	E	R	G
E	I	H	K	E	Y	O	U
T	D	I	S	P	L	A	Y

2 ☆☆ **Complete the sentences with words from Exercise 1.**

1 Oh, no! A *strap* on my backpack has broken.
2 There's a problem with the ________ on my phone. It's very dark.
3 These photos have turned out badly because the ________ on my camera was dirty.
4 Let's carry this bag together. You take one ________ and I'll take the other.
5 Where's the ________ for the saucepan?
6 Is this the ________ for charging your phone?
7 This ________ on my laptop is for changing the audio volume.
8 The ________ of this book looks really great, but the book wasn't very interesting!
9 You need to attach this ________ to the printer.

3 ☆☆☆ **Write a description of a "mystery object." Use at least four of the words from Exercise 1. Send your description in an email to a classmate, or ask them to guess the object in the next class.**

It has a display and it has one or two buttons, but it doesn't have a plug. It doesn't have a handle, but it has a strap. What is it?

____
____
____
____
____

A Conversation

2.01 **4** ☆ **Listen to a conversation about the past between Katie and her grandma. Mark (✓) the things they mention.**

1 a plug ☑

2 a calculator ☐

3 a video cassette ☐

4 a TV ☐

5 a camera ☐

6 a PowerPoint presentation ☐

5 ☆ **Underline the key words in the sentences. (See the *Learn to Learn* tip in the Student's Book, p26.)**

1 Katie is going to <u>work on a history project</u>. *F*
2 Her grandma thinks that young people spend too much time using "technological things." ___
3 Katie's grandma didn't use a calculator in school. ___
4 There weren't many shows on TV before. ___
5 Katie thinks that life before sounds fun. ___
6 When her grandma was in school, each student had a small blackboard to write on. ___

2.01 **6** ☆☆ **Listen again. Are the sentences in Exercise 5 *T* (true) or *F* (false)?**

7 ☆☆☆ **What three modern inventions could you not do without?**

____
____

GRAMMAR IN ACTION

Past Perfect with *Never, Ever, Already, By (Then), By the Time*

1 ★ **Read the sentences and underline the action that happened first.**

1 I had already had lunch when my sister arrived.
2 My sister had already gotten married by the time she was 20.
3 Dan wasn't happy because I had turned down his invitation.
4 By the time the game ended, we had scored five goals!
5 We had walked a very long way by the time we found the river.

2 ★★ **Match the beginnings of the sentences (1–5) with the ends (a–e).**

1 I had never seen snow [c]
2 We had only been at the hotel a few minutes when [ ]
3 Had you ever run more than 5 km [ ]
4 By the time my grandpa settled in the U.S.A., [ ]
5 We had already been to six different stores [ ]

a by the time Clara decided to buy something.
b before today?
c before I went to Sierra Nevada.
d he'd lived in six different countries.
e the storm started.

3 ★★ **Put the words in the correct order to make sentences.**

1 car / seen / had / the / already / .
I had already seen the car.
2 had / then / back / by / come / .
Jack ______
3 called / woken up / you / I / when / already / ?
Had ______
______
4 Europe / never / year / had / last / been / I / to / .
Before ______
5 then / a snake / ever / you / before / seen / ?
Had ______
______

4 ★★ **Complete the sentences with the simple past or the past perfect form of the verbs in parentheses.**

1 Pablo had never taken (never / take) guitar lessons before he gave (give) his first concert.
2 ______ (Sean / ever make) lasagna before yesterday?
3 School ______ (already / start) when I ______ (arrive).
4 By the time Sara ______ (leave) England, she ______ (learn) to speak English very well.
5 I ______ (never / feel) real terror until I ______ (see) that movie!
6 ______ (everyone / already / go) to bed by the time the fire ______ (start)?

5 ★★★ **Complete the text with the simple past or the past perfect form of the verbs in parentheses.**

Emma [1] moved (move) to a new school last year. By the time she [2] ______ (be) there a couple of weeks, she [3] ______ (already / settle) down very well. And now things are going even better! Last week, she [4] ______ (become) the captain of the school soccer team.

She [5] ______ (be) very happy about this because she [6] ______ (always / want) to be the team captain. And yesterday she [7] ______ (receive) her exam results. More good news! She [8] ______ (never / get) such good grades before!

6 ★★★ **Complete the sentences with your own ideas. Use the past perfect.**

1 Before this year, I ______
2 We didn't win the game because we ______
______
3 I signed up for karate lessons because ______
______
4 By the time Ella finished college, ______
______
5 Alan was going through a hard time because ______
______

WRITING
An Opinion Essay

1 ☆ **Look at the essay quickly. Does the writer think that life used to be better in the past?**

____

2 ☆☆ **Read the essay and answer the questions. Mark (✓) and circle the correct answers.**

1 In which TWO paragraphs does the writer give ideas to support their opinion?
A ☐ B ☐ C ☐ D ☐

2 In paragraph A, the writer …
a asks the reader a question.
b gives their opinion.

3 In paragraph D, the writer …
a repeats their opinion.
b asks the reader a question.

3 ☆☆ **Complete the essay with the *Useful Language* phrases in the box.**

~~first~~ in addition in conclusion second therefore this means that

4 ☆☆ **What different words or phrases does the writer use to avoid repeating items 1–4 below?**

1 in the past (paragraph B)
____

2 better (paragraph B)
____

3 situation (paragraph B)
____

4 look at (paragraph D)
____

5 ☆☆ **Complete the sentence.**

In paragraphs B and C, to describe life in the past, the writer uses the simple past, __________, and __________.

Did Life Use To Be Better?

A Older people often say that, in the past, life used to be better. However, in my opinion, this is simply not true.

B [1] ___First___, let's look at the situation of women. In the old days, many men (and some women) used to think that a woman's role in life was to be a mother and to do the housework and the cooking. Fortunately, attitudes have changed a lot since then! [2] __________ women today are in a much more favorable position.

C [3] __________, the number of very poor people around the world has decreased significantly in the last 20 or 30 years. [4] __________, healthcare has improved in poor countries. In the past, many children would die when they were still very young in those places. This happens far less often now. [5] __________, we can talk about huge change in two very important areas.

D [6] __________, the world today is a much better place. If we examine the facts, no one would want to go back to "the golden past." This past only exists in some people's imaginations. It never existed in reality.

PLAN

6 ☆☆ **Write an opinion essay. Look at the statement. Write down three reasons why you agree or disagree with it.**

It's more important to speak English today than in the past.

____
____
____

WRITE

7 ☆☆☆ **Write your opinion essay. Remember to include four paragraphs and examples of *used to*, *would*, the simple past, the past perfect, and the *Useful Language* phrases from Exercise 3.**

CHECK

8 **Do you …**
- give your opinion?
- give reasons for your opinion?
- summarize your opinion?

2 REVIEW

VOCABULARY

1 Rewrite the second sentence so that it has a similar meaning to the first. Use the phrasal verbs in the box and any other words you need.

do without	go back	go through	look forward to	move to	settle down	try out	turn down

1 Let's return to the bus station.
Let's ______________________ the bus station.

2 I'm very excited about the concert on Saturday.
I'm ______________________ the concert on Saturday.

3 I have to take a shower every morning.
I can't ______________________
every morning.

4 I'm sorry, but I can't accept your invitation.
I'm sorry, but I have to ______________________ .

5 Mike's adapting well to life in Milan.
Mike's ______________________ in Milan.

6 Beth isn't enjoying life at all right now.
Beth is ______________________ a hard time right now.

7 Jose used to live in California, but he went to live in New York.
Jose ______________________ New York.

8 Let's see what this new video game is like!
Let's ______________________ video game!

2 Complete the crossword. Use the picture clues.

Down ↓

1
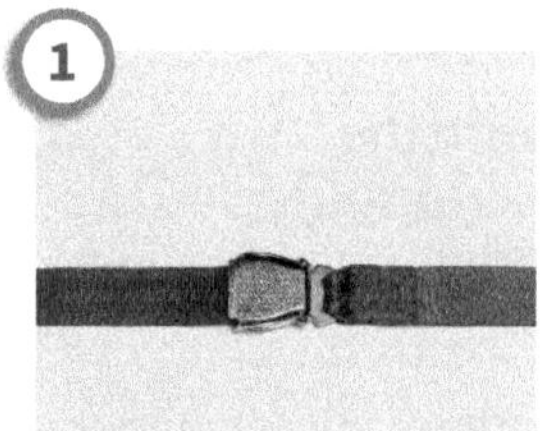

2
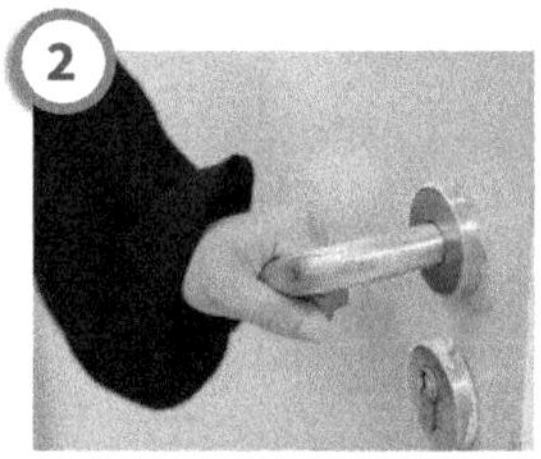

3

6

7
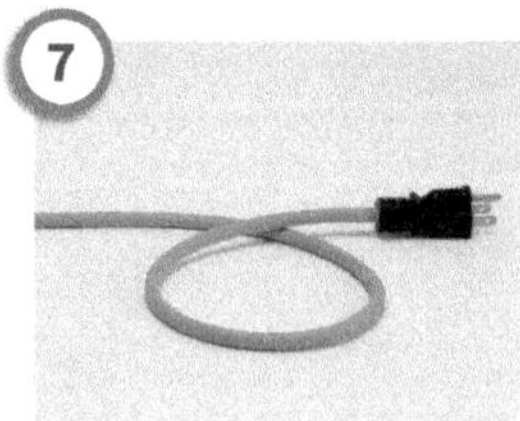

8
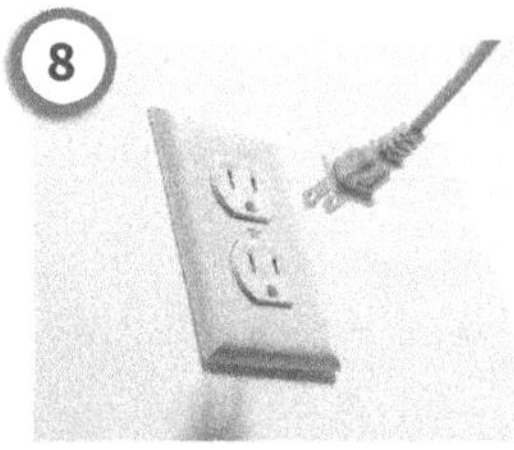

Across →

4

5

7

9

GRAMMAR IN ACTION

3 **Circle the correct answer.**

When my mom was ten, she [1]*got / would get* a cat for her birthday. She [2]*would love / loved* the cat, and it used to follow her everywhere. The cat [3]*did explore / would explore* other people's yards, and it [4]*didn't fight / used to fight* with other cats from time to time. Then one day, the cat [5]*didn't come / used to come* home. Mom [6]*used to be / was* so sad – she [7]*put up / would put up* posters to try and find it. Finally, it came home five days later. Mom was very happy!

4 **Circle the sentence (a or b) that has a similar meaning to the first.**

1 The train had already left when we got to the station.
  a When we got to the station, the train left.
  b We arrived at the station late, so we missed the train.

2 Before we went to Brazil last year, I'd never been there.
  a Last year was the first time I was in Brazil.
  b I didn't visit Brazil last year.

3 By the time I learned to drive, I'd spent a lot of money on driving lessons.
  a I spent a lot of money before I could drive.
  b I learned to drive before I spent a lot of money.

4 Amy hadn't finished her homework when Aidan came.
  a Aidan arrived and Amy finished her homework.
  b When Aidan came, Amy was still doing her homework.

5 Ryan had never seen a lion before he went to the zoo last week.
  a Ryan didn't see a lion at the zoo.
  b Before his trip to the zoo last week, Ryan hadn't seen a lion.

6 We had taken a lot of photos by the time our vacation was over.
  a We took a lot of photos on vacation.
  b When our vacation ended, we took a lot of photos.

CUMULATIVE GRAMMAR

5 **Complete the text with the missing words. Circle the correct options.**

Joe said, "I [1]_____ to this new school a month ago, but I [2]_____ down to life here very well."
"[3]_____ through a hard time?" I asked him.
"Yes, I [4]_____," he said. "It's been [5]_____ difficult. At my old school I [6]_____ a lot of friends. And I [7]_____ them very often after school. Before I came here, I [8]_____ that it would be so hard to make new friends. It's been [9]_____ harder than I thought."
"[10]_____ up for any school clubs?" I asked.
"Yes, I [11]_____ to two or three different ones," Joe replied. "You know, I [12]_____ really popular at my old school," he continued. "Nothing like this [13]_____ to me before."

1 a moved b had moved c used to move
2 a didn't settle b haven't settled c hadn't settled
3 a Did you go b Had you gone c Have you been going
4 a did b have c been
5 a far b absolutely c really
6 a would have b used to have c have had
7 a had seen b have been seeing c would see
8 a hadn't expected b haven't expected c wouldn't expect
9 a pretty b totally c far
10 a Did you sign b Have you signed c Had you signed
11 a 've been going b had gone c would go
12 a used to be b would be c 've been
13 a had happened b has happened c has been happening

3 What's usually on your plate?

VOCABULARY
Cooking Verbs

1 **Find 11 more verbs for cooking in the word search.**

C	H	O	P	O	(P	E	E	L)
R	O	V	G	R	I	L	L	D
I	S	E	A	S	O	N	S	I
S	P	R	E	A	D	O	L	B
H	O	C	R	A	M	F	I	O
A	R	O	A	S	T	F	C	I
R	E	O	V	E	R	R	E	L
B	A	K	E	M	Y	Y	O	T
O	M	U	G	R	A	T	E	E

2 **(Circle) the verb that goes with the food.**

1 (*grate*) / *peel* cheese
2 *bake* / *boil* water
3 *peel* / *season* an apple
4 *grate* / *roast* a chicken
5 *spread* / *roast* butter
6 *chop* / *slice* bread
7 *grate* / *fry* eggs
8 *peel* / *overcook* fish

3 **Complete the sentences with the words in the box.**

bake chop grill ~~overcook~~ season spread

1 Please don't *overcook* the meat. One or two minutes is enough.
2 ________ the onions into small pieces.
3 Do you often ________ bread in the oven?
4 When you barbecue, you ________ meat over a fire.
5 ________ the dish with salt and pepper.
6 Do you have a knife to ________ the jam?

4 **Complete the recipe with the words in the box.**

fry grate overcook season ~~slice~~ spread

A Fantastic Snack

[1] *Slice* some bread and toast it. Take some refried beans and [2] ________ them on the bread. [3] ________ some cheese and put it on the refried beans. In a pan, heat up some oil. Then put an egg in the pan and [4] ________ it for only one or two minutes. Don't [5] ________ it! Put the egg on the bread. [6] ________ with black pepper. It's ready to eat!

5 **Write how to make something simple (e.g., an omelet, a milkshake, your favorite sandwich).**

____

____

____

____

6 **Write the adjective form of the verbs from Exercise 1. (See the *Learn to Learn* tip in the Student's Book, p35.)**

Add *-ed*	Add *-d*	Irregular
peeled		

Explore It!

Guess the correct answer.

What is the main ingredient of this dish called Bombay Duck?

a duck b horse meat c fish

Find another interesting fact about food or a special dish. Write a question and send it to a classmate in an email, or ask them in the next class.

READING

An Online Forum

1 ☆ **Match the photos 1–4 with the four comments on the online forum A–D.**

2 ☆☆ **Complete the article with the missing sentence parts a–f.**

a The food was OK

b and they read some poems

c because it's so incredibly beautiful

d My sister doesn't eat meat

e ~~The highlight of the trip was when we went to an underwater restaurant~~

f in the summer

3 ☆☆ **Read the text and check the meaning of the words in the box in a dictionary. Then complete the sentences.**

~~costume~~	freezing	highlight
hiking	melt	practical

1 What *costume* are you going to wear in the school play?

2 Riding your bike at night without lights is not ________ at all.

3 Eat your ice cream quickly or it'll ________!

4 My friend Mia goes ________ even in the middle of winter!

5 It's ________ outside, so put on a warm coat.

6 The ________ of the meal was when they brought out my birthday cake.

4 ☆☆☆ **Which of the four places would you most like to eat at? Why? Write three or four sentences.**

____

____

____

____

____

____

____

1 

2 

3 

4 

ASK IT!

HOME ANSWER NOTIFICATIONS SEARCH

Where's the most memorable place you've ever eaten?

A My dad won $100,000 in the lottery, and he decided to do something very practical with it: he took all of us on vacation to the Maldive Islands! (They're about 640 kilometers southwest of India.) [1] *e*. Beautiful tropical fish swam past as we ate! It was an experience that I'll never forget! [2] ________ but nothing special.

Sam, Toronto

B In northern Finland, there's a fantastic snow hotel with a restaurant made of ice! It's only open in the winter. Perhaps it melts [3] ________! You need to wear warm clothes or you're going to be freezing because you sit on ice chairs all the time! We had grilled salmon (very good!), but the roasted meat for the main course was a bit overcooked. Oh, well, nowhere's perfect!

Oona, Helsinki

C When we were on vacation in Ireland, we went for a medieval dinner at Bunratty Castle. It was a lot of fun! They had actors in traditional costumes, [4] ________. There was also Irish music. The food was good, but we didn't eat with our hands like in medieval times! They had vegetarian food, too. [5] ________ and she loved the baked carrots with grated cheese.

Charlotte, Denver

D The most memorable place I've eaten was Pulpit Rock in Norway. The meal wasn't exactly spectacular – a sandwich, an energy bar, and an apple! But the view *was* spectacular! You could see for miles! And the food didn't taste bad after hiking for a couple of hours! It's not easy to get to Pulpit Rock from Ireland. But I might go back a second time [6] ________!

Conor, Dublin

GRAMMAR IN ACTION

Future Forms

1 ☆ **Match the verbs in sentences 1–6 with the uses a–c.**

1 We're meeting at six o'clock. [c]
2 The bus leaves at 10 a.m. [ ]
3 I'm going to study more this year. [ ]
4 Are you and Luis playing tennis tonight? [ ]
5 The restaurant opens at 7 p.m. [ ]
6 Zoe's going to try to make lasagna. [ ]

a to talk about future plans and intentions
b to talk about scheduled or timetabled events
c to talk about fixed arrangements in the future

2 ☆☆ **Circle the correct options.**

1 What *do you do* / (*are you doing*) tonight?
2 The game *starts* / *is starting* in five minutes!
3 My sister *learns* / *is going to learn* to drive next year.
4 We *meet* / *'re meeting* in the park at six o'clock.
5 I *make* / *'m going to make* dinner in a few minutes.
6 Joel *has* / *is going to have* a piano lesson in a few minutes.
7 I*'m getting* / *'m going to get* my green belt in judo this year. It's my big goal for the year.
8 We *go* / *'re going* skateboarding this weekend.

3 ☆☆☆ **Write about two fixed future arrangements that you have or haven't made and two future intentions that you have or don't have.**

____
____
____
____

4 ☆ **Match the underlined verbs in sentences 1–3 with the uses a–c.**

1 Those cookies smell amazing. And I'm sure they're going to taste delicious! [ ]
2 More people will become vegetarians in the future. [ ]
3 I might want some more pizza. Let me finish this first! [ ]

a a future prediction that we don't feel sure about
b a future prediction based on evidence in the present
c a future prediction that we feel sure about

5 ☆☆ **Complete the predictions with *be going to*, *will*, or *may/might*, and the verbs in the box.**

come	have	love	~~miss~~	not cost	not finish

1 Oh, no! It's 5:59! We *'re going to miss* the six o'clock train!
2 John ________ to the party. Let's wait and see!
3 I'm sure Deborah ________ the present you chose for her. You have great taste.
4 This meal ________ a lot! Prices are cheap!
5 Some experts say that one day everyone in the world ________ enough food to eat.
6 I ________ this book tonight, but I'm going to try.

6 ☆☆☆ **Complete the conversation with the correct form of the verbs in parentheses. Use the simple present, present continuous, *be going to*, *will*, or *may/might*.**

A I [1] *'m never going to cook* (never / cook) a big meal again!
B Why? It wasn't so bad. And I'm sure your cooking [2] ________ (get) better in the future.
A Hmm … I suppose I [3] ________ (make) some progress.
B Don't be so negative! Anyway, what [4] ________ (you / do) after lunch?
A I [5] ________ (go) to the movies with Will. The movie [6] ________ (start) at 5 p.m.

7 ☆☆☆ **Complete the sentences with your own ideas.**

1 In ten years, I might ________________.
2 In 100 years, everyone will ________________.
3 I might ________________.

VOCABULARY AND LISTENING

Quantities

1 ☆ **Circle the correct quantity to describe each photo.**

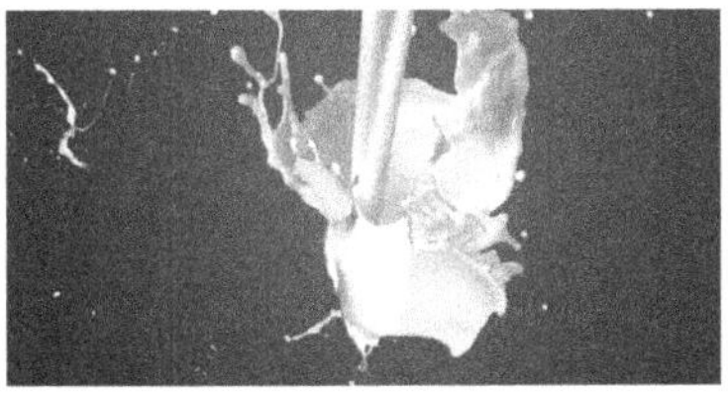

1 a splash / *cup* of milk

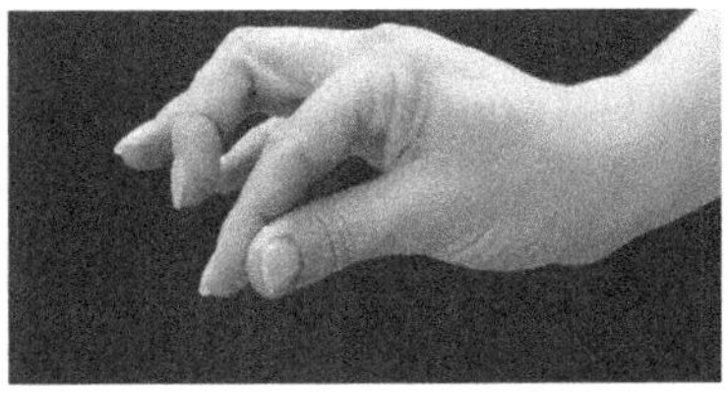

2 a *bag* / *pinch* of salt

3 a *spoonful* / *bag* of sugar

4 a *slice* / *piece* of bread

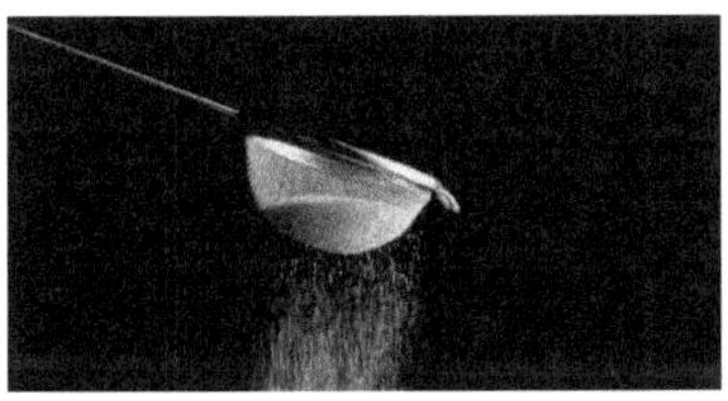

5 a *sprinkle* / *handful* of sugar

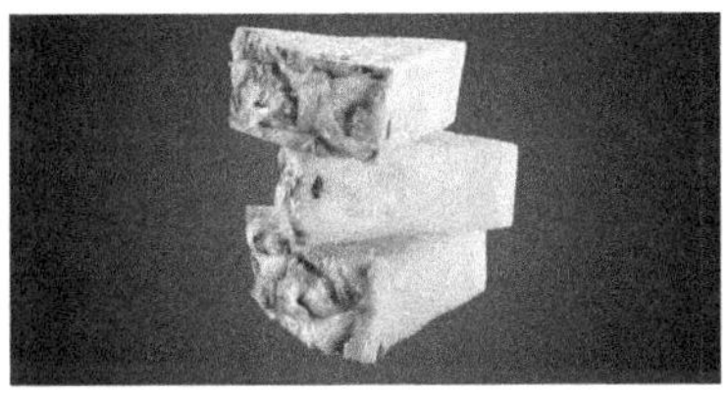

6 *cups* / *chunks* of pineapple

2 ☆☆ **Complete the chart with the quantities in the box. (See the *Learn to Learn* tip in the Student's Book, p38.)**

a bag of   a cup of   a handful of   a piece of
a pinch of   a slice of   a splash of   a spoonful of
a sprinkle of   ~~chunks of~~

Sugar	Milk	Cheese
		chunks of

3 ☆☆☆ **Write about three things you like to eat or drink. Use the quantities from Exercise 2.**

I love two slices of toast and jam for breakfast.

An Interview

3.01 **4** ☆ **Listen to a man talking about his job. Are the sentences *T* (true) or *F* (false)?**

1 James has his own food store. ___
2 James works a lot. ___
3 His job has several good points. ___
4 He never has time to eat the food that he cooks. ___

3.01 **5** ☆☆☆ **Listen again and complete the sentences with ONE word from the interview.**

1 James works in the city of Chicago.
2 In the restaurant, there can be ______ people eating at the same time.
3 The food needs to arrive at customers' tables quickly and the dishes need to be of ______ quality.
4 James doesn't ______ down very often while he's working.
5 It's a profession for people who are ______.
6 It's very different from an ______ job.
7 The opinion of the ______ is important to James.
8 It's important to ______ the food.

6 ☆☆☆ **Would you like to do James' job? Why / Why not? Write three or four sentences.**

GRAMMAR IN ACTION

Future Continuous and Future Perfect

1 ☆ Complete the sentences with the verbs in parentheses in the future continuous.

1 I ___'ll be reading___ (read) this book all evening.
2 He ______________ (listen) to the podcast later.
3 I ______________ (not lie) on the sofa all afternoon!
4 My parents ______________ (not work) this time tomorrow.
5 ______________ (we / eat) at two o'clock?
6 ______________ (Ryan / cook) for a long time?

2 ☆☆ Look at Carmen's diary. Complete the sentences with the correct future continuous form of the verbs in parentheses and short or long answers.

Monday	Tuesday	Wednesday
tennis (5 p.m.)	homework (morning)	dance class (6 p.m.)

1 She ___'ll be playing___ (play) tennis at 5 p.m. on Monday.
2 She ______________ (not do) homework on Tuesday afternoon.
3 She ______________ (start) her dance class at 6 p.m. on Wednesday.
4 A ______________ (Carmen / play tennis) on Monday?
B ______________
5 A What day ______________ (she / take) her dance class?
B ______________

3 ☆ Circle the correct options.

1 I'm going to bed very late tonight. I *'ll* / *won't* have gone to bed by 11 p.m.
2 I hope that I *'ll* / *won't* have learned to drive in a few years. I think it would be fantastic!
3 My mom works in another country. By tomorrow, I *'ll* / *won't* have seen her for two months.
4 My dad often cooks for the family. He *'ll* / *won't* have cooked several meals for us by the end of this week.
5 **A** Will you have become a doctor by the time you're 20?
B That's impossible! *Yes, I will.* / *No, I won't.*

4 ☆☆ Complete the conversation with the verbs in the box in the future perfect and short answers.

arrive grill ~~make~~ not fry not have slice

A [1] ___Will___ you ___have made___ lunch by one o'clock?
B No, [2] ______________. Why?
A The guests [3] ______________ by then!
B Oh, no! I [4] ______________ the potatoes to make the fries, but I [5] ______________ them.
A And [6] ______________ you ______________ all the meat?
B No, [7] ______________. I [8] ______________ time!

5 ☆☆ Circle the correct time expression.

1 I'll be sleeping *in two hours* / *since next week*.
2 Will you be sitting by the pool *this time tomorrow* / *since the time you were 18*?
3 We'll have finished all our exams *by the end of this month* / *for three hours*!
4 *Next Tuesday* / *By the end of this year*, we'll have visited five different countries!
5 We'll be eating that roasted chicken *in five minutes* / *by the time it's cooked*.

6 ☆☆☆ Use the future continuous or future perfect to write about things that you will do or hope that you will do.

1 By the end of this year, ______________.
2 At nine o'clock tonight, ______________.
3 Next weekend, ______________.
4 By the time I'm 30, ______________.

WRITING

A Listicle

1 ☆ **Look at the listicle quickly. What is it about?**

2 ☆☆ **Read the listicle. Are the sentences *T* (true) or *F* (false)?**

1 Tight clothes will be popular. F
2 We will need to buy new clothes more often. ___
3 We will wear very different shoes from today. ___
4 We'll have less choice when we buy clothes. ___
5 Clothes will become intelligent. ___

3 ☆☆☆ **Rewrite the sentences with the underlined *Useful Language* phrases in the listicle.**

1 More information here soon!
Watch this space!
2 Smart clothes will be the usual thing we wear.
3 I can't imagine anything more exciting than being a fashion designer.
4 T-shirts will always be popular. *(three expressions)*

FIVE FUTURE FASHION TRENDS!

1 Baggy clothes will be everywhere!

Comfortable baggy clothes will be the norm as the planet gets hotter. Tight denim jeans will have gone completely out of style by 2030, and clothes made of cool cotton will be in all the stores.

2 Clothes will wear out more quickly!

Fast fashion will mean that most clothes will only last five or six months. Clothes will become cheaper as a result.

3 Sneakers are here to stay!

People of all ages wear sneakers nowadays, and that isn't going to change. If you ask me, sneakers will be around forever. I love sneakers, so what could be better news than that?

4 Clothes to match eyes and hair color!

Very soon, we won't just be buying clothes by size. You'll be able to buy clothes to match your eyes or hair color. Everything will be personalized. Watch this space!

5 High-tech clothes!

We already have smartphones, and they aren't going anywhere. But soon we'll have smart clothes, too! They'll adapt to our body temperature and even to our size! The future's going to be exciting!

PLAN

4 ☆☆ **Write your own listicle. Take notes in your notebook on the theme "Five ways my life will be different in 20 years." Use the spidergram to generate ideas.**

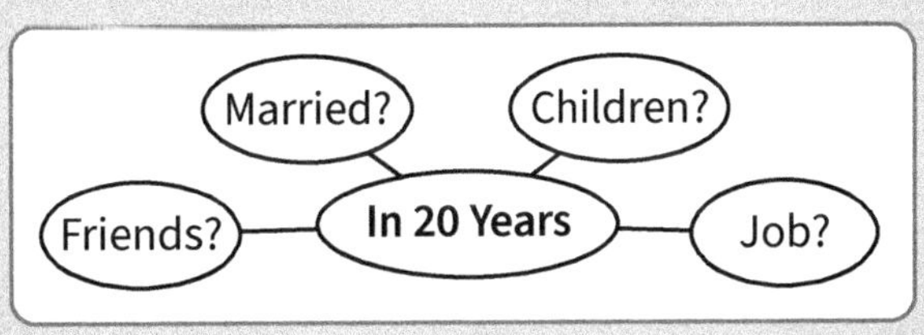

WRITE

5 ☆☆☆ **Write your listicle. Remember to include future forms, vocabulary from this unit, and phrases from the *Useful Language* box (see Student's Book, p41).**

CHECK

6 **Do you ...**

- explain what you will or might be doing in the future?
- explain what will be normal in the future?
- make any other predictions?

3 REVIEW

VOCABULARY

1 Complete the crossword. Use the clues.

ACROSS →

4 ________ an egg
5 ________ an apple
6 ________ bread
7 ________ chicken
9 ________ a cake
11 ________ sausages

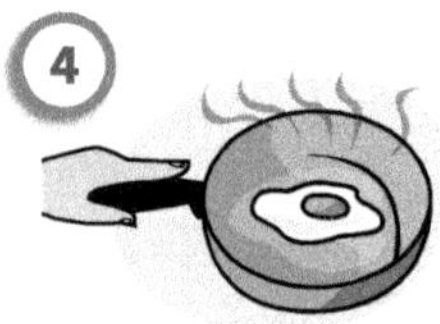

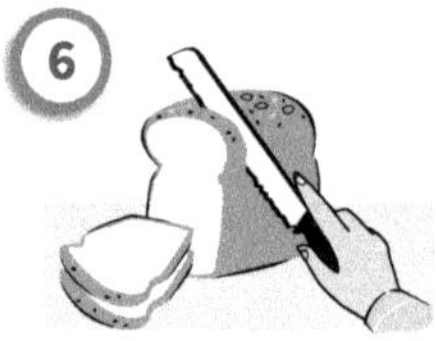

DOWN ↓

1 ________ onions
2 ________ a veggie burger
3 ________ cheese
6 ________ meat
8 ________ butter
10 ________ water

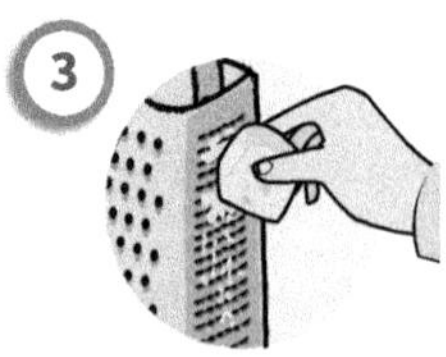

2 Circle the correct options.

1 a cup of *sugar* / *fish*
2 a piece of *salt* / *chocolate*
3 a slice of *cake* / *milk*
4 some chunks of *yogurt* / *cheese*
5 a handful of *nuts* / *milk*
6 a bag of *water* / *chips*
7 a pinch of *pepper* / *chicken*
8 a sprinkle of *potatoes* / *grated cheese*
9 a spoonful of *apples* / *olive oil*
10 a splash of *vinegar* / *salt*

GRAMMAR IN ACTION

3 Circle the correct options.

1 What time *does* / *will* the movie start?
2 I *will* / *'m going to* make pizza for the first time next weekend.
3 *Do you go* / *Are you going* to the market with Sean this weekend?
4 Dad *might* / *will* be late for dinner tonight. It depends on when he finishes work.
5 I think that in the future people *will eat* / *are eating* less meat.
6 My cousin *will stay* / *is staying* at my house tonight.

4 Complete the predictions with the future perfect or future continuous form of the verbs in parentheses.

Space Predictions

- In 20 years, scientists [1] ________ (discover) a new planet in our solar system.
- People [2] ________ (live) on Mars by the end of this century.
- A big asteroid [3] ________ (not hit) the Earth by the end of this millennium.
- People [4] ________ (go) to the moon for their vacations in 50 years.
- We [5] ________ (not find) intelligent life in the rest of the universe by the end of this century.
- Scientists [6] ________ (plan) journeys outside the solar system very soon.

CUMULATIVE GRAMMAR

5 Complete the text with the missing words. Circle the correct options.

Teen Fashion: Past, Present, and Future

Teenagers [1] ______ clothes especially designed for them for long. Before the 1950s, they [2] ______ their own fashion, and clothing companies [3] ______ about making special clothes for them. In the past, young teenagers [4] ______ children's clothes, and teenagers that were [5] ______ older wore adults' clothes. Clothes for teenagers [6] ______ a lot since then! It's [7] ______ hard to predict what kind of clothes teenagers [8] ______ in the future because fashion changes very quickly. They [9] ______ wear high-tech clothes, or perhaps they [10] ______ 1960s hippie-style clothes soon. Who knows? Two things are [11] ______ clear, though – fashion designers [12] ______ very good at inventing new teen styles in the past, and they [13] ______ to continue doing this in the future, too.

	a	b	c
1	weren't wearing	haven't been wearing	haven't worn
2	didn't use to have	wouldn't have	weren't having
3	have never thought	would never think	had never thought
4	have been wearing	would wear	were wearing
5	a bit	really	a far
6	had changed	have changed	have been changing
7	extremely	a lot	absolutely
8	are wearing	will have worn	will be wearing
9	will	might	're going to
10	wear	're wearing	'll be wearing
11	pretty	a lot	far
12	are	have been	had been
13	are trying	will have tried	are going to try

4 How do you use your senses?

VOCABULARY

The Five Senses

a

b

c

d

e

1 ☆ **Match the sentences 1–5 with the pictures a–e.**

1 It sounds good. [e]
2 It looks amazing! [ ]
3 It smells good. [ ]
4 It feels nice. [ ]
5 It tastes great. [ ]

2 ☆☆ **Complete the sentences with the correct form of *feel*, *look*, *smell*, *sound*, or *taste*, and *like* if necessary.**

1 That song ___sounds___ good. Who is it?
2 I love this ice cream. It ________ fantastic!
3 You ________ a movie star in those sunglasses!
4 Can you give me a massage? Oh, that ________ so good!
5 Please open the window. It doesn't ________ good in here!
6 Do I ________ an American when I speak English?
7 This bread ________ cardboard! It's very dry!
8 The sky ________ dark. I think it's going to rain.

3 ☆☆ **Complete the chart with your own ideas. Write three things for each column. (See the *Learn to Learn* tip in the Student's Book, p47.)**

It Feels Good	It Looks Good	It Smells Good	It Sounds Good	It Tastes Good
a cat's fur				

4 ☆☆☆ **Write four sentences about what you experienced with your senses yesterday. Use *feel*, *look*, *smell*, *sound*, or *taste*, and *like* if necessary.**

My new shoes looked good.

____

____

____

Explore It!

Guess the correct answer.

How far away can elephants smell water?

a 5 km b 12 km c 19 km

Find another interesting fact about animal senses. Write a question and send it to a classmate in an email, or ask them in the next class.

THE BEST JOB IN THE WORLD?

HOME | **STORIES** | PHOTOS

For most of us, eating chocolate is a pleasure. But for Alice Schaffer, it's much more than that – it's a full-time job! Alice, you see, works for an important food company, and she eats their chocolate to see how it tastes. Before she worked there, she didn't have a **background** in food science. She was, in fact, working as a salesperson. Then one day, a neighbor told her that her company was looking for people to work as taste-testers. Alice immediately thought, "That sounds like a great job! And I might be good at it because I love chocolate!" So she applied and ... they gave her the job! Of course, it isn't enough to like chocolate if you want to get a job tasting chocolate. You need to be able to identify and **accurately** describe different **flavors** and textures. And that's something you can't learn – you're either born with it or you aren't.

When Alice tells people what she **does for a living**, they often look surprised because they imagine that she must spend all day eating chocolate. But her job isn't really like that at all. When she tastes the chocolate from a bar, she just eats a little piece. You don't need to eat the whole bar to know what it tastes like! The hardest part of the job is when she tastes something that isn't 100 percent right. The **challenge** is to describe exactly what's wrong with the taste. The food technicians need this precise information so they can investigate the problem.

Alice is extremely **proud** of her job, and it's easy to see why: there can't be many people in the world whose job helps give so much pleasure to others!

READING

A Magazine Article

1 ★ **Read the magazine article quickly. What is Alice Schaffer's job?**

a She makes chocolate.
b She checks the taste of chocolate.
c She sells chocolate.

2 ★★ **Match the words in bold in the article with the definitions.**

1 feeling pleasure because you've done something well proud
2 particular tastes ____
3 someone's past situation ____
4 correctly, without making any mistakes ____
5 does to earn money ____
6 something that needs effort or might be hard to do ____

3 ★★ **Read the text again. For each question, circle the correct option.**

1 What is the writer trying to do in this article?
a explain how to get a job as a chocolate taster
b write a biography of Alice Schaffer
c describe what a chocolate taster does
d tell the reader about the professional life of Alice Schaffer

2 What kind of useful experience had Alice had before?
a She had worked as a salesperson.
b She had studied food science.
c She hadn't really had any experience.
d Her neighbor had taught her about the job.

3 What is the principal quality you need to be a chocolate taster?
a dedication b natural talent c to love chocolate d to write very well

4 What is the most difficult part of the job?
a giving precise information when the quality isn't good
b not eating the chocolate
c people not thinking it's a serious job
d working with the food technicians

5 What might Alice say to a friend about her job?
a It's an easy job.
b I love my job!
c There's often a lot of stress in my job.
d The chocolate is bad for me.

4 ★★★ **Would you like to do Alice Schaffer's job? Why / Why not?**

____

GRAMMAR IN ACTION

Modals of Deduction and Possibility

1 ☆ **Match the sentences 1–3 with their meanings a–c.**

1 I'm sure it's nice to work as a chocolate taster. ☐
2 Perhaps it's nice to work as a chocolate taster. ☐
3 I'm sure it isn't nice to work as a chocolate taster. ☐

a It can't be nice to work as a chocolate taster.
b It must be nice to work as a chocolate taster.
c It might be nice to work as a chocolate taster.

2 ☆☆ **Look at the sentence *It might be nice to work as a chocolate taster.* Which two modal verbs can we use in place of *might*, without changing the meaning?**

____

3 ☆ **Circle the correct options to describe the pictures.**

1

He *can't* / (*must*) be tired.

2
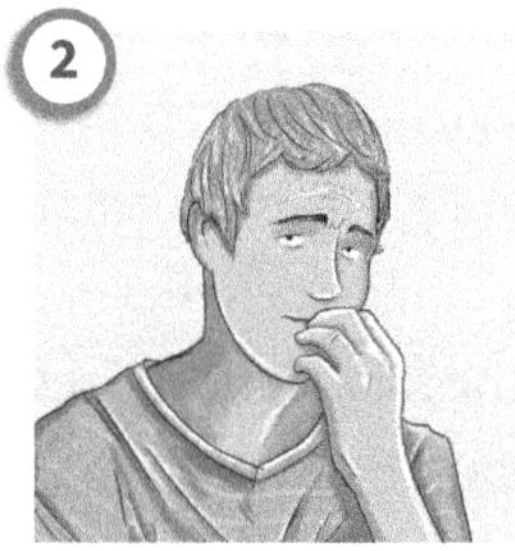

He *can't* / *must* feel relaxed.

3

That car *can't* / *must* be expensive!

4
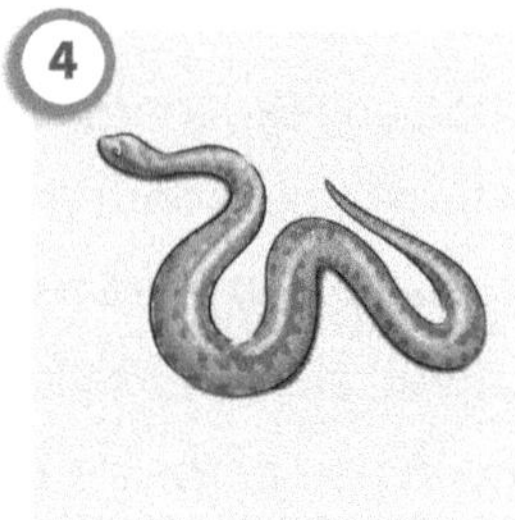

Careful! It *might* / *must* be dangerous.

5

It *can't* / *must* be raining.

6

They *may* / *can't* still have some good bargains.

4 ☆☆ **Complete the conversation about the photo with *must*, *might*, or *can't*.**

A Look at this photo! What is it?
B It [1] __might__ be a house!
A No, it [2] ________ be! How would you get in?
B It [3] ________ be a fake photo. You never know …
A No, the photo's real. I think it [4] ________ be art or something. There [5] ________ be another explanation. I'm sure the artist is famous.
B Perhaps … you [6] ________ be right. The person who designed it [7] ________ be very creative!

5 ☆☆☆ **Rewrite the sentences so that they have the same meaning. Use *must*, *might*, *may*, *could*, or *can't*.**

1 Perhaps Nathan's still at school.
Nathan might/may/could still be at school.
2 I'm sure that isn't the right answer.
____
3 I'm sure you need good exam results to study medicine in college.
____
4 This is possibly the worst movie I've seen!
____
5 I'm sure it doesn't take a long time to make that dish.
____

6 ☆☆☆ **Write deductions about these situations. Use *must*, *might*, *could*, or *can't*.**

1 Edison is a professional soccer player.
He must be very fit.
2 All the stores are closed.
____
3 Your phone isn't working.
____
4 Everyone is looking at the sky.
____

VOCABULARY AND LISTENING

Describing Texture, Sound, Taste, Etc.

1 ☆ **Complete the adjectives.**

1 spic y
2 rou __ __
3 shin __
4 fain __
5 color __ __ __
6 sou __
7 smoo __ __
8 shar __
9 smell __
10 transpar __ __ __

2 ☆☆ **Write an appropriate adjective from Exercise 1 before the nouns.**

1 spicy curry
2 dirty, ________ socks
3 nice, ________ skin
4 ________ cream
5 ________, new scissors
6 ________ flowers

3 ☆☆ **Complete the sentences with adjectives from Exercise 1.**

1 A crocodile has very sharp teeth.
2 This sauce is too ________ for me. My mouth's burning!
3 Can you pass the sugar? This yogurt is very ________.
4 Does this cake have bananas in it? I can detect a ________ taste of them, but it's not very strong.
5 This lotion is great! My hands feel so ________!
6 This metal box looks very ________ when it's in the sun.
7 Tom's chin felt ________ because he hadn't shaved.

4 ☆☆☆ **Write short descriptions of the items in the box. Use at least one adjective from Exercise 1 in each description. You can use affirmative or negative verbs.**

apple	cats	my favorite food	snakes

1 ________
2 ________
3 ________
4 ________

An Interview

5 4.01 ☆ **Listen to an interview about the senses. According to Simon Redding, which of our senses is the most important?**

a hearing ☐
b sight ☐
c smell ☐
d touch ☐

6 4.01 ☆☆ **Listen again. For each question, (circle) the correct option.**

1 Simon says that some people …
  (a) can't smell very much.
  b use sight and smell well.
  c feel cold all the time.
2 What does Simon say about dreams?
  a Some people open their eyes when they dream.
  b It's good to have colorful images.
  c Taste and smell are not usually part of dreams.
3 When we are communicating, we …
  a shouldn't only be listening.
  b need to smile.
  c shouldn't be negative.
4 What has the biggest impact on us in a conversation?
  a how well the other person listens
  b how the other person moves and looks at us
  c the language that the other person uses
5 What would Simon Redding like people to do?
  a depend on their eyes to understand better
  b remember to use all of their senses
  c close their eyes and feel objects

7 ☆☆☆ **Think about what you have done today. When have you used each of the five senses?**

____
____
____
____
____

GRAMMAR IN ACTION

Obligation, Prohibition, Necessity, and Advice

1 ★★ **Circle the correct options.**

How to Use Music to Relax

- ♩ You [1]*should* / *don't need to* listen to calm music.
- ♩ You [2]*don't have to* / *must not* listen to heavy metal. It's not relaxing!
- ♩ You [3]*ought to* / *shouldn't* sit in a comfortable position.
- ♩ You [4]*need to* / *must not* concentrate on the music.
- ♩ To help you concentrate, you [5]*don't need to* / *should* close your eyes.
- ♩ You [6]*shouldn't* / *don't need to* be with other people when you listen to the music. It's far better if you are alone.
- ♩ You [7]*must not* / *don't need to* wear headphones, but it's better if you have them.

2 ★★ **Complete the the interview with a perfume maker with the missing words. Circle the correct options.**

A [1]_____ study a lot before you became a perfume maker?

B Yes, I [2]_____. I [3]_____ study chemistry for four years.

A And I suppose that a perfume maker [4]_____ to have a good sense of smell!

B Yes, of course. You [5]_____ consider becoming a perfume maker without that! And you [6]_____ to be very patient because it takes a long time to create the right smell. And you [7]_____ copy other people. That's bad! You [8]_____ to be original!

	a	b	c
1	Must you	Should you	(c) Did you have to
2	must	have	did
3	had to	need to	ought to
4	must	should	needs
5	should	shouldn't	don't have to
6	must	need	don't have
7	must not	don't need to	should
8	must	have	should

3 ★★★ **Rewrite the sentences with *must*, *should*, *need*, or *have to*.**

1 I recommend that you see a doctor.
You should see a doctor.

2 It's not permitted to walk on the grass.

3 There's no obligation for us to watch the game.

4 Antonio didn't have an obligation to give me a present.

5 It's necessary for us to contact him.

6 Being in the sun without a hat is not recommended.

Past Obligation

4 ★★★ **Put the words in the correct order.**

1 had / exams / yesterday / two / to / I / take / .
I had to take two exams yesterday.

2 didn't / have / She / year / walk / last / to / school / to / .

3 party / had / Miguel / to / so / study, / didn't / the / go / he / to / .

4 have / people / to / tickets / Did / buy / ?

WRITING

An Encyclopedia Entry

Marlee Matlin, August 24, 1965

1 Marlee Matlin is an actress. She is the only deaf actress who has won an Oscar.

2 Marlee was born in 1965 and grew up in a small town near Chicago. At the age of 18 months, she lost almost all her hearing. She acted for the first time at the age of seven in a production of *The Wizard of Oz* with actors who were all deaf. In 1986, she won the Oscar for best actress at the age of only 21. In the movie, she didn't have to speak. She played the role of a deaf woman who refuses to speak because the rest of the world refuses to learn sign language.

3 Marlee has appeared in many movies and TV shows, including *Sesame Street.* She isn't just famous as an actress; she is also known as an enthusiastic worker for many charities.

4 Marlee can speak quite well, and she doesn't always need to use an interpreter because she can read people's lips. According to her autobiography, she never planned to become an actress. She thought there wouldn't be any opportunities for deaf people.

1 **Read the encyclopedia entry. What is Marlee's occupation?**

______

2 **Complete the sentences with information from the encyclopedia entry.**

1 She was born in 1965.
2 When she was seven, ______.
3 In the movie where she won an Oscar, her character was ______.
4 She is also famous as ______.
5 She can read people's lips, so ______.
6 When she was young, she used to think that ______.

3 **Complete the sentences with the underlined *Useful Language* in the encyclopedia entry.**

Javier Bardem, March 1, 1969

Javier Bardem [1] grew up in Madrid, but he [2] ______ in Las Palmas in the Canary Islands. In his career, he has acted in many movies, [3] ______ *Skyfall*, a James Bond movie. He actually appeared in his first movie [4] ______ only six. [5] ______ Bardem, he originally wanted to be a painter, but he didn't have enough talent. Outside of movies, Bardem is [6] ______ a firm defender of ecological causes.

PLAN

4 **Write an encyclopedia entry. First, take notes in your notebook about your favorite actor, fictional character, or athlete.**

- Name and date of birth
- A short general description
- Information about their life
- An interesting fact

WRITE

5 **Write your entry. Remember to include four paragraphs, vocabulary from this unit, and phrases from the *Useful Language* box (see Student's Book, p53).**

CHECK

6 **Do you ...**

- include the person's name and date of birth?
- include information about the person's life?
- include information about the person's work?

4 REVIEW

VOCABULARY

1 Complete the sentences with the correct form of *feel* (*like*), *look* (*like*), *smell* (*like*), *sound* (*like*), or *taste* (*like*).

1 It doesn't ________ very good in here. Please open the windows.

2 When you sing, you don't really ________ an angel!

3 Wow! That photo ________ a painting! It's so artistic!

4 **A** Do you want to go skateboarding?
  B Yes, that ________ a good idea!

5 This perfume ________ roses and oranges. It's great!

6 It ________ an oven in here! Please turn the air conditioning on!

7 This strawberry ice cream ________ great! Did you make it yourself?

8 These tomatoes ________ really green, and they ________ really hard.
  So, I don't think they're going to ________ very good!

2 Complete the crossword. Use the clues.

Down ↓

1 There's a ________ taste of lemon in this cake, but it isn't very strong.

2 That sweater is ________. You need to wash it.

3 I like the feel of this leather. It's very ________.

5 Be careful – it's very ________! Don't cut yourself!

Across →

2 If you have a stomachache, you shouldn't eat ________ food.

3 I love Chinese food, especially sweet and ________ chicken.

4 That bird is very ________. It looks beautiful.

5 The metal buttons on your coat look very ________ under these lights.

6 A rhinoceros has hard, ________ skin.

GRAMMAR IN ACTION

3 Complete the conversation with *might*, *must*, or *can't*.

A Is the new *Mission Impossible* movie good?

B I haven't seen it yet, but it [1]________ be pretty good. It has four stars in the newspaper.

A You never know, it [2]________ be awful.

B You [3]________ be serious! They spend a lot of money to make those movies. So, it [4]________ be fantastic!

A Hmm, you [5]________ be right. But it [6]________ be as good as the last one. That's the best movie I've ever seen.

B You [7]________ be surprised. David's seen it and he couldn't stop talking about it!

A Really? Then it [8]________ be great! David and I always agree about movies!

4 Complete the sentences with the correct form of *must* (*not*), (*not*) *need to*, *should*, or (*not*) *have to*.

1 You ________ touch the paintings. It's not allowed!
2 We ________ get up early this morning because the train left at seven o'clock.
3 I don't think you ________ wear green with purple, but it's your decision.
4 I ________ borrow your bike, but thanks for the offer.
5 ________ you ________ wear a uniform at your old school?
6 I ________ clean up my bedroom tonight, but I'm not going to do it.
7 You ________ help me, but it'd be great if you could.
8 ________ we ________ get a visa to travel to Argentina?

CUMULATIVE GRAMMAR

5 Complete the conversation with the missing words. Circle the correct options.

CHRIS What [1] ____ this weekend?
TOM I [2] ____ any plans yet.
CHRIS What about this new Sensorium exhibition? It [3] ____ be good. You never know.
TOM I [4] ____ to it! It was so interesting that I [5] ____ about it all the time. It [6] ____ be the best exhibition I've ever been to. I'm [7] ____ sure about that. I [8] ____ that going to museums to look at paintings was boring. But this exhibition is different because you listen to music and smell things while you're looking at each painting. I [9] ____ that an exhibition could be like that! You [10] ____ go, Chris! You [11] ____ disappointed!
CHRIS Thanks! I [12] ____ miss it! By next Monday, both of us [13] ____ it!

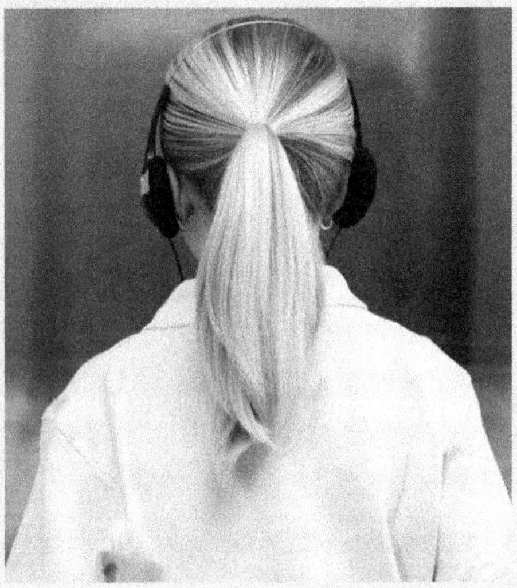

	a	b	c
1	do you do	will you do	are you doing
2	don't make	haven't made	haven't been making
3	might	must	will
4	'd already been	may have been	've already been
5	've been thinking	've thought	think
6	can	needs to	must
7	pretty	absolutely	far
8	would think	used to think	've been thinking
9	've never imagined	might never imagine	'd never imagined
10	should	don't have to	'll
11	can't be	won't be	haven't been
12	won't	don't need to	aren't going to
13	will see	will have seen	will be seeing

EXAM TIPS: Listening Skills

Listening: Multiple-Choice Pictures

You will listen to short extracts and choose from different options. This tests your ability to listen for specific information and answer questions about what you hear.

Exam Guide: Multiple Choice

- If the question is about a conversation between a boy and a girl, underline which of the two people you need to answer the question about. For example: *What food will the boy eat?*
- Decide if the question is asking about the past, present, or future. The verb tense and time expressions in the question will help you. For example: *What is the weather like now?* is a completely different question from *What will the weather be like tomorrow?*
- Listen carefully to see if the meaning is positive or negative. For example: *Can you buy some fruit – but not bananas?* tells us that the speaker does not want bananas.
- Usually the answer will come in the middle or at the end of the listening and not at the beginning. This means that you should always wait until the end of each listening before you choose your answer.

REMEMBER!

Don't choose a picture as an answer just because you hear information about it in the listening. Usually you will hear information related to all three pictures!

Listening Practice: Multiple-Choice Pictures

Tip!

Listen for key words and synonyms to help you identify the answer.

1 Choose the correct meaning for the expressions.

1 Are you kidding me?
   A I don't believe you.   B That's interesting!
2 You're getting on my nerves.
   A You're funny!   B You're irritating me!
3 You'll never know unless you try.
   A You should try.   B Are you going to try?
4 You're coming to my party, aren't you?
   A Are you sure you're coming to my party?
   B Can you confirm that you're coming to my party?
5 You must feel really proud of your exam results!
   A I'm sure you feel really happy about your exam results.
   B You ought to feel very happy about your exam results.
6 I get a lot out of playing chess.
   A Playing chess is hard for me.   B I really enjoy playing chess.

E.01 **2 You will hear six short extracts. Are the sentences *T* (true) or *F* (false)?**

1 The boy's sister irritates the girl. ___
2 The speaker says everyone should study abroad. ___
3 The boy's coffee is very hot. ___
4 There is a present in the box. ___
5 Some fruit tastes better than it smells. ___
6 The girl thinks going to college is a bad idea. ___

Tip!

Sometimes information later in the listening will contradict or correct the information before. For example:

A *Amy loves skateboarding.*

B *Well, that was before her accident. She hasn't done it since then.*

This is another reason why you need to wait until the end before choosing your answer.

E.02 **3 Listen to the conversation between Ben and his mom. Answer *Yes* or *No*.**

1 Are the dishes washed? ______
2 Does Ben need to do his homework tonight? ______
3 Is Ben going to speak to his friends tonight? ______

E.02 **4 Listen again. What is Ben going to do first? Choose the correct option A, B, or C.**

A

B

C

EXAM TIPS: Reading Skills

Reading: Multiple Matching

Matching People with Activities and Things

You will read descriptions of people and match them with the best options. Remember that there are more options than people, so read carefully! The extra options usually fit only partially, not completely.

Exam Guide: Multiple Matching

- Begin by reading the five descriptions of the people. Underline the key information in each description.
- Next, read all eight texts carefully and underline the key information in each one.
- Then compare the underlined information in the description of the first person with the underlined information in the texts. Which text is the best match for this person?
- Don't choose a text just because it repeats some words from the description of one person. You need to focus on the meaning of the descriptions and the texts and not on individual words.

REMEMBER!

Be very careful when choosing – the text needs to be a perfect match for everything the person wants.

Reading Practice: Multiple Matching

Identifying Meaning

1 **Choose the option (A, B, or C) that shows the meaning of the first sentence.**

1 Jack wants to do without chocolate for a week.
   - A Jacks wants to eat less chocolate for seven days.
   - B Jack thinks he can do without chocolate for seven days.
   - C Jack would like not to eat chocolate for seven days.

2 Chloe is looking forward to learning to drive.
   - A Chloe plans to learn to drive.
   - B Chloe is happy that she will start learning to drive soon.
   - C In the future, Chloe will learn to drive.

3 Liam has moved to Veracruz.
   - A Liam is living in Veracruz now.
   - B Liam has traveled to Veracruz.
   - C Liam is spending some time in Veracruz.

Synonyms

2 **Match the <u>underlined</u> words with the synonyms in the box. There are four extra words.**

be born	can	cook in oil	cook in an oven	cut into pieces
heat	know	lived as a child	think	will possibly

1 I'm going to bake a cake. ______
2 Jon grew up in Chicago. ______
3 How long does it take to fry the onions? ______
4 Rachel might go to college. ______
5 I guess they must be brother and sister. ______
6 You need to chop the peppers. ______

Tip!
Don't look for words that match exactly. Read the text carefully and underline synonyms of the key information words.

Eliminating Options

3 **Read what Laura wants. Then decide which options A–D you can eliminate.**

Laura wants to buy a new phone. It must be the latest model, feel very light and smooth, and have a very large display.

A We repair all the latest models of phones …
B Our store has a good selection of phones, including classic old models …
C We have the latest models. They're very light, and have big displays. We're definitely the best place to get a new watch.
D This store specializes in all sorts of digital devices. Its products are expensive, but they look great!

Tip!
When you think you have a correct answer, check the incorrect options again to be sure that they don't match.

Finding Differences

4 **Read about Sam and Nathan. Find three differences between them.**

Sam wants to try out some new recipes. He cooks every day. During the week, he doesn't have much time to cook, but he has time on the weekend to make more complicated dishes. He doesn't eat fried food or food with a very strong flavor.

Nathan likes very spicy food. He wants to buy a book of recipes. He is especially interested in making quick meals in the frying pan.

______
______
______

EXAM TIPS: Listening Skills

Listening: Fill in the Blanks

You'll have to listen and complete notes or sentences. The notes or sentences summarize what you hear. You have to write a word, number, or very short noun phrase in each blank.

Exam guide: Fill in the Blanks

- Pay attention to the instructions. They remind you what you have to do, but more importantly, they tell you what the topic is.
- After the instructions, there is a pause. Use this to read the notes or sentences.
- While you read, try to think about what type of information is missing. It might be a day, a number, a date, or a price, for example.
- The sentences or notes summarize what the speaker says, so you are not going to hear what is written on the page. Pay attention to the key words.
- As you listen, fill in the blanks – remember the answers are one word, a number, or a very short phrase.
- During the second listening, check your answers.

REMEMBER!

Check that your answers make sense in the context if you are given a second opportunity to listen.

Tip!

The sentences and notes will give you clues about what type of information is missing. Read everything carefully.

LISTENING PRACTICE: Fill in the Blanks

1 **Read the notes. What type of information is missing?**

Rent a Bus
Number of seats on our bus: [1] ______
Bus leaves: 10:30 a.m.
Meet at youth club: [2] ______
Price of exhibition entrance: $7
Special group price (over 20 people): [3] $______

E.03 **2** **You will hear some information about a visit to a photography exhibition. Listen and write the correct answer in the blanks (1–3) in Exercise 1. Then listen again and write down the other numbers that you hear.**

______

Tip!

What you read in the questions is not what the person says – it is a summary or paraphrase. Think about the meaning and listen for key words.

3 E.04 **Listen and complete the sentences.**

A Angela's mom told her that her ______________ had won the contest many years ago.

B To find out more about the contest, visit the website – www______________org.

C Angela entered the contest with her ______________ .

D The class was given a grant of $ ______________ to build their robot.

4 **You will hear an announcement about events coming up at a youth club. Before you listen, read the notes in Exercise 5. What type of information is missing from the blanks?**

a type of clothing	a day	the name of a food	a number	a subject	a time

5 E.05 **Listen and complete the notes with one or two words or a number, date, or time.**

Youth Club Events: November

Weekly cooking classes:

Every [1] ______________ at 5 p.m.

Mary

1) bake a chocolate cake; 2) roast [2] ______________

Visit 1:

Date: Friday, the 16th at [3] ______________ p.m.

Helen Fields – fashion designer

Workshop: match colors; choose jeans; decorate a plain white [4] ______________ (must bring)

Visit 2:

Date: Saturday, the 24th at 7 p.m.

Dr. Michael Redding – professor of [5] ______________

Talk: history of logos

Logo contest:

1st prize [6] $______________ in cash

Past and Present, Simple and Continuous

- We use the **simple present** to talk about facts, habits, and routines.
  My sister likes pizza.
  I don't read every day.
- We use the **simple past** to talk about completed events and actions in the past.
  I translated the text into Spanish for him.
  I visited Madrid three years ago.
- We use the **present continuous** to talk about actions that are happening now or around now.
  That girl over there is waving at me.
- We use the **past continuous** to talk about actions in progress around a time in the past. We also use ***when*** and ***while*** to mean "during that time," or to connect two events happening at the same time.
  Isabella was wearing a dress last night.
  While I was looking for the dog, he was looking for the ball.

Present Perfect and Simple Past

- We use the **present perfect** when something started or happened in the past and continues to be true until now. We can say how long something has been true but not when it started.
  I've been to Barcelona. (When isn't specified, but it continues to be true.)
  They've been sightseeing. (We don't know when.)
  She's wanted to talk to you since she arrived. (She continues to want to.)
- We use the **simple past** when the moment in which something happened has ended. When it happened isn't always mentioned, usually because it is clear.
  I went to Barcelona in June.
  They went sightseeing yesterday.
  She wanted to talk to you.

GRAMMAR PRACTICE

Past and Present, Simple and Continuous

1 Circle the correct options.

1 I (cut) / *was cutting* my finger yesterday.
2 *Do you go* / *Are you going* to the supermarket now?
3 What *happens* / *is happening* when you push this button?
4 Mary *listened* / *was listening* to music when I *saw* / *was seeing* her.
5 You *don't need* / *aren't needing* to pack a lot of clothes.
6 *Did you buy* / *Were you buying* some bread for a sandwich?

2 Complete the conversation with the correct form of the verbs in parentheses.

MOM Harry, you're going to be late. What [1] *are you doing* (you / do)?
HARRY I [2] ________ (try) to find my keys!
MOM Where [3] ________ (you / normally / leave) them?
HARRY I always [4] ________ (put) them on my desk. But they're not there now.
MOM When [5] ________ (you / have) them last?
HARRY I [6] ________ (have) them in my hand when I [7] ________ (arrive) here yesterday. I [8] ________ (talk) to Jonah on the phone.
MOM Oh, yes, I [9] ________ (remember). You [10] ________ (go) into the living room.
HARRY I [11] ________ (look) there, but I [12] ________ (not find) them.
MOM [13] ________ (you / wear) your coat?
HARRY Yes, I was. Maybe I [14] ________ (leave) them in my coat pocket. Here they are!

Present Perfect and Simple Past

3 Complete the sentences with the present perfect or simple past form of the verbs in the box.

not laugh	not play	paint	~~see~~	sing	tell

1 *Have* you *seen* Scarlett? She's looking for you.
2 Pete ________ very well at the concert yesterday.
3 I ________ you 100 times! Don't call me Timmy!
4 Don't touch the door. They ________ just ________ it.
5 Why ________ you ________ at that joke? It was really funny.
6 Lucas ________ soccer for a month. He's injured.

4 Put the words in the correct order to make sentences.

1 sent / Has / photo / you / Erin / the / ?
Has Erin sent you the photo?
2 tennis / I / liked / you / didn't / know / playing / .
____
3 long / your / taken / a / You / time / to / essay / have / finish / .
____
4 questions / the / didn't / exam / all / answer / on / the / We / .
____
5 you / us / did / Why / come / with / to / decide / ?
____
6 heard / from / We / news / Julia / any / haven't / .
____

GRAMMAR REFERENCE

UNIT 1

Present Perfect Simple

- We use the **present perfect** to talk about actions, experiences, and facts in the past when the exact time is not mentioned or important.
  I've found my favorite T-shirt.
  She has been to the mall.

Present Perfect Continuous

	Affirmative	Negative
He / She / It	has been practicing for years.	hasn't been eating very well.
I / We / You / They	have been practicing for years.	haven't been eating very well.

Questions		
Has	he / she / it	been sleeping a lot?
Have	I / we / you / they	

Short Answers		
Yes,	he / she / it	has.
	I / we / you / they	have.
No,	he / she / it	hasn't.
	I / we / you / they	haven't.

- We use the **present perfect continuous** to talk about an action or a series of actions that started in the past, is still in progress, and we expect to continue.
  I've been studying hard all week.
  She's been exercising since last summer.
- We often use the **present perfect continuous** to say how long we have been doing something.
  I've been taking piano lessons for nine years.
- We use the **present perfect continuous** to focus on the ongoing action rather than the result.
  We've been preparing for the party all day!
- We don't use the **present perfect continuous** with stative verbs (e.g., *like, have,* and *know*).
  Emily has liked him since she met him.
  (NOT ~~*Emily has been liking him since she met him.*~~)
  We have had our cat since she was a kitten.
  (NOT ~~*We've been having our cat since she was a kitten.*~~)
- We form the **present perfect continuous** with **subject** + ***has/have*** (***not***) + ***been*** + ***-ing***.
  I've been playing basketball since I was seven.
  She's sick, so she hasn't been coming to school this week.
- We form **present perfect continuous** questions with ***has/have*** + **subject** + ***been*** + ***-ing***.
  Has she been living here for a long time?

Present Perfect Simple and Present Perfect Continuous

- We use the **present perfect simple** to emphasize that the action or event is recently finished. We use the **present perfect continuous** for actions or events that are still going on up to now.
  I've studied for my English test tomorrow.
  (completed action)
  I've been studying for my English test tomorrow.
  (ongoing)

Modifiers

- We use **modifiers** with adjectives to make the meaning stronger and show emphasis. Common modifiers include *a bit, a little, a lot, totally, really, absolutely, extremely, pretty, fairly,* and *far.*
  He was really upset.
  I felt extremely sorry for him.
  Her parents are pretty strict.
  She can't do anything.
  They work extremely hard.
  They need to relax.
  Her room is really messy.
  There's stuff everywhere!

GRAMMAR PRACTICE

Present Perfect Simple

1 Complete the sentences with the present perfect simple form of the verbs in parentheses.

1 I _haven't worn_ (not wear) this dress since last spring!

2 Paul ________ (wait) all his life for this moment.

3 ________ Jane ________ (tell) you what happened yesterday?

4 We ________ (not play) this computer game for months.

5 Our school ________ (organize) a fashion show.

Present Perfect Continuous

2 Complete the sentences with the present perfect continuous form of the verbs in the box.

clean ~~listen~~ rain run wear

1 I _'ve been listening_ to this great radio station on my phone.

2 Your face is red. ________ you ________?

3 It ________ all morning, so we can't go out.

4 Her feet hurt because she ________ those high-heeled boots all day.

5 Vanessa ________ her room all morning – it was a mess!

Present Perfect Simple and Present Perfect Continuous

3 Circle the correct options.

1 How many times have you (seen) / *been seeing* this movie?

2 I've *folded* / *been folding* all my clothes, and they're in my suitcase now.

3 Have you *sent* / *been sending* the photos to me yet?

4 Dad's tired because he has *painted* / *been painting* all day.

5 Daniel hasn't *read* / *been reading* Laura's message yet, so don't tell him what she said.

6 I've *ordered* / *been ordering* pizza – it'll be here in a few minutes.

4 Complete the conversation with the present perfect simple or continuous form of the verbs in parentheses.

TIM Hi, Mia. I [1] _haven't seen_ (not see) you all day. What [2] ________ (you / do)?

MIA Oh, hi, Tim. I [3] ________ (study) for an exam. It's history. I [4] ________ (always / find) it hard to study history.

TIM Me, too. I [5] ________ (even / not start) yet. I [6] ________ (try) to write that essay for English class. I [7] ________ (not finish) it yet, though.

MIA I have. Do you want to see it? I [8] ________ (write) about my last vacation. I'm really happy with it.

TIM That's funny. I [9] ________ (do) the same thing. Maybe the teacher's going to think we [10] ________ (copy) each other!

Modifiers

5 Circle the correct options.

1 I'm not buying these jeans. They're *absolutely* / (*much too*) big for me.

2 The movie was *really* / *totally* good and *a bit* / *extremely* funny.

3 Lydia's dress was *totally* / *a lot* amazing, and her brother looked *pretty* / *a little* handsome.

4 These jeans are *a bit* / *pretty* shorter than those jeans.

6 Match the beginnings with the endings.

1 The exam was really — e
2 I'm really
3 Diego thought the story was fairly
4 Edwin's party was a lot more
5 Liam takes totally amazing
6 The food was pretty

a fun than Carl's party last month.
b good, but I didn't like the music.
c sorry, but I can't talk now.
d amusing, but nobody else liked it.
e difficult, but I think I passed.
f photos, but he never shares them.

GRAMMAR REFERENCE

UNIT 2

Used To, *Would*, and Simple Past

- ***Used to*** emphasizes that past states, habits, and actions are now finished.
  It used to be a castle, but now it's a museum.
  She used to play piano. Nowadays, she just sings.
- ***Used to*** does not have a present form. For present habits and states, we use the simple present.
  My cousin visits us every summer.
  (NOT ~~*My cousin use to visit us every summer.*~~)
- We use ***used to*** and ***would*** to talk about habits and actions in the past that are different today.
  They used to run on Tuesdays, but now they run on Fridays.
  When I was young, my parents would take me for a walk every day.
- We also use ***used to***, but not ***would***, to talk about states and feelings in the past that are different today.
  My grandfather used to have black hair, but now it's white.
  (NOT ~~*My grandfather would have black hair …*~~)
  She used to love volleyball, but she doesn't play anymore.
  (NOT ~~*She would love volleyball …*~~)
- We do not use ***used to*** or ***would*** to talk about things that only happened once or to say how many times something happened.
  Last year, I went to Mexico.
  (NOT ~~*Last year, I used to go to Mexico.*~~)
  Yesterday, I called my dad three times.
  (NOT ~~*Yesterday, I would call my dad three times.*~~)
- We put question words at the beginning of the question.
  What things did you use to do when you were younger?
- We don't often use ***would*** in questions and negative sentences.
- ***Used to*** is like any regular verb. The past tense ends in ***d***, but in questions and negative forms, the verb does not end in ***d***.
  I used to like playing, but I didn't use to like practicing.
  Did you use to have a bike when you were younger?

Past Perfect with *Never*, *Ever*, *Already*, *By* (*Then*), *By the Time*

- We use the **past perfect** with other past tenses to talk about actions or states that happened before the main past action or state.
  We hadn't seen the news, so we didn't know about the storms.
  I couldn't call you on Friday because I had left my phone at home.
- We use **adverbs** and **adverbial phrases** such as *already, never, ever, by the time,* and *by then* with the past perfect.
- ***Already***, ***never***, and ***ever*** come before the past participle, but ***yet*** comes at the end of the sentence.
  We had never been to New York until last year.
  They've gone to school, but they haven't had breakfast yet.
- We use ***already*** to emphasize that something had happened.
  I had already finished my test before class was over.
- If something had happened ***by the time*** something else happened, it happened before it.
  They had already heard the news by the time I told them.
- If something had happened ***by then***, it happened before then.
  I finally arrived at the party, but by then all the food had gone.

GRAMMAR PRACTICE

Used To, *Would*, and Simple Past

1 Complete the sentences with *used to* and the verbs in parentheses.

1 I didn't use to like (not like) wearing dresses when I was younger.

2 Edwin ____________ (eat) a lot of candy until his dentist told him to stop.

3 Adela ____________ (not look) forward to PE classes because she wasn't very fit.

4 Our soccer team ____________ (win) every game, but now they're terrible!

5 My dad ____________ (not have) a cell phone when he was 15.

6 My teachers ____________ (not give) us much homework.

2 Make questions with *used to* or the simple past. Sometimes both are possible.

1 When / Helen / buy / this car / ?

When did Helen buy this car?

2 there / always / be / a movie theater here / ?

____

3 your dad / have / a bike / when he was a teenager / ?

____

4 you / hear / what happened yesterday / ?

____

5 What types of music / you / listen to / when you were younger / ?

____

3 Choose the correct sentences. Sometimes both are correct.

1 (a) When she younger, my aunt used to live in Miami.
 b When she was younger, my aunt would live in Miami.

2 a When I was five, I wouldn't eat vegetables.
 b When I was five, I didn't use to eat vegetables.

3 a There used to be a lot more stores on this street.
 b There would be a lot more stores on this street.

4 a My dad used to have a long beard.
 b My dad would have a long beard.

Past Perfect with *Never*, *Ever*, *Already*, *By (Then)*, *By the Time*

4 Circle the correct options.

1 I was excited because I'd (never) / *already* been to a wedding before.

2 Had the teacher *already* / *never* started the class when Paul arrived?

3 By *then* / *the time* you called, it was too late to do anything.

4 When the movie started, they'd *never* / *already* eaten all the pizza.

5 I started running, but *by then* / *by the time*, the man had disappeared.

6 When we took my grandmother to Los Angeles, she had *never* / *ever* flown before.

5 Complete the text with the words in the box.

already	by	had	had already	~~never~~	then

I was very nervous. I'd [1] never played the guitar in front of people before. I walked onto the stage. [2] ____________ the time I'd picked up the guitar, my hands were shaking. They [3] ____________ turned the lights off, so I couldn't really see much. I put the strap around my neck, but by [4] ____________, the rest of the band had [5] ____________ started playing the first song! I put my hands on the guitar to play ... and there was no sound. Someone [6] ____________ pulled the plug!

6 Use the prompts to write simple past and past perfect sentences.

1 They / not sleep / all night because / there / be / a big storm

They hadn't slept all night because there was a big storm.

2 By the time we / get / there, our team / score

____

3 I / try / to cancel my order yesterday, but by then, / they / already send / it

____

____

4 Until last week, Camilla / never / speak / in English

____

5 When you / arrive, / Dennis / already / find / his keys

____

Future Forms

- We use ***be going to*** to talk about future plans and intentions and predictions that we feel sure about.
  After I graduate, I'm going to travel the world.
  My sister is going to stay with my grandparents this summer.
  I'm going to feel sick if I eat all of that!
- We use ***will*** to talk about what is going to happen in the future, especially things that you are certain about or things that are planned.
  I'll see him tomorrow.
  I won't cook later – I'll be out.
- We use ***may*** (***not***) or ***might*** (***not***) instead of ***will*** (***not***) to show that we feel less sure about a future action or event but think it is probable.
  I might not go to college.
  I may get a job with my dad.
  When he gets here, he may want to speak to you.
  Don't call after ten o'clock – we may be watching a movie.

Present Continuous for Future

- We use the **present continuous** to talk about future arrangements when the time is fixed.
  They're getting married this summer.
  What are you doing this weekend? – I'm going shopping with my parents.
  She isn't coming to the party. She's spending the day with her cousins.

Simple Present for Future

- We use the **simple present** to talk about events that are scheduled or timetabled.
  The lesson starts at 9:30 tomorrow instead of 10:30.
  They don't go back to school until next Monday.

Future Continuous

Affirmative/Negative		
I / You / He / She / It / We / You / They	will	be flying this time next week.
I / You / He / She / It / We / You / They	won't	

Questions		
Will	I / you / he / she / it / we / you / they	be flying this time next week?

Short Answers		
Yes,	I / you / he / she / it / we / you / they	will.
No,	I / you / he / she / it / we / you / they	won't.

- We form the **future continuous** with ***will*/*may*/*might*** + **be** + ***-ing***.
- We use the **future continuous** to talk about actions we believe will be in progress at a future time.
  In five years, he'll be living in Veracruz and working as a teacher.
  By 2025, everyone will be wearing smartwatches.
- We can also use the **future continuous** to talk about future plans.
  I'll be leaving at 2 p.m. I'm picking my little brother up from school, so I can't be late.
- We put question words at the beginning of a question.
  What will you be doing in 20 years?
  When will computers be cooking dinner for us?

Future Perfect

Affirmative/Negative		
I / You / He / She / It / We / You / They	will have finished	the project by 2050.
I / You / He / She / It / We / You / They	won't have finished	

Questions			
Will	I / you / he / she / it / we / you / they	have finished	the project by 2050?

Short Answers		
Yes,	I / you / he / she / it / we / you / they	will.
No,	I / you / he / she / it / we / you / they	won't.

- We form the **future perfect** with ***will*** + ***have*** + **past participle**.
- We use the **future perfect** for actions that will be completed before a certain time in the future.

GRAMMAR PRACTICE

Future Forms

1 Circle the correct options.

1 Mike's not sure yet, but he *'s going to* / *might* get a new bike.

2 Do you think it *'s going to* / *might* be a sunny day tomorrow?

3 Some scientists say the world's temperature *will* / *going to* rise by four degrees in the next ten years.

4 Enjoy your vacation. I'm sure you *'ll* / *might* have a great time.

5 Tracy is certain she *is going to* / *might* study biology in college. It's her favorite subject.

6 I'm not feeling very well, so I *may not* / *won't* go to the game. I'll text you later.

2 Complete the sentences with the correct future form of the verbs in parentheses.

1 This restaurant ___doesn't open___ (not open) until 5 p.m. this evening.

2 Do you think you ________ (pass) all your classes?

3 What time ________ (Tim / meet) us tomorrow?

4 I've decided I ________ (not buy) a new printer.

5 Larry hasn't decided yet, but he ________ (not have) dinner with us.

6 I ________ (order) pizza at the restaurant tonight.

3 Complete the conversations with the correct form of the verbs in the box.

buy need ~~overcook~~ start

1 A Can I help you with dinner?
B Yes. You fry the chicken because I ___'ll___ probably ___overcook___ it!

2 A Where are you going?
B Into town. I ________ a new coat.

3 A What time do you want to meet?
B The concert ________ at 8 p.m., so let's say 7:30.

4 A Is there enough food for everyone?
B I don't know. I think we ________ more bread.

Future Continuous and Future Perfect

4 Complete the sentences with the future continuous form of the verbs in parentheses.

1 What ___will you be doing___ (you / do) this time tomorrow?

2 My jeans are dirty, so I ________ (not wear) them tomorrow.

3 The music teacher says she ________ (not teach) us how to play this song.

4 While you're working hard, I ________ (enjoy) myself on vacation.

5 You can't meet him later; you ________ (write) your English essay.

6 Tomorrow's a national holiday, so we ________ (prepare) a special meal!

5 Complete the text with the future perfect form of the verbs in the box.

drink eat laugh see ~~sleep~~ spend

What do humans do in one year? By this time next year, you [1] ___will have slept___ for 2,372 hours and you [2] ________ over 1,000 hours on the Internet. You [3] ________ probably ________ some funny things, which means you [4] ________ for a total of 36.5 hours. If you're American, you [5] ________ around 46 slices of pizza, and you [6] ________ probably ________ well over 800 liters of water.

6 Correct the mistake in each sentence.

1 This time tomorrow, I'll ~~have~~ lying on the beach in Italy. ___be___

2 In 20 years, we'll be built robots to do the cooking for us. ________

3 By the time tomorrow, I'll have finished all my exams. ________

4 I be not doing anything later, so call me. ________

5 Will have you started dinner when I get home? ________

6 What will be you wearing to Itzel's party? ________

Modals of Deduction and Possibility

- We often use ***can***, ***can't***, ***could***, ***may***, ***might***, and ***must*** + **infinitive without *to*** to say how possible or probable we think an action or event is.
  It can't be him! He never wears a hat to a party!
  She's late. She might be stuck in traffic.
  You must be tired after your long trip.
- We use ***can*** to make general statements about possibilities.
  They say that drinking too much coffee can be bad for you.
  Try drinking more water; it can help you feel more awake!
- We use ***can't*** to say that we think something is impossible or cannot be true.
  That can't be Samantha. She's in China!
  They can't be at home. I saw them leaving an hour ago.
- We use ***could***, ***may***, and ***might*** to say we think something is possible.
  You could have an infection; that's why you're feeling bad.
  A *Who's that man?*
  B *I don't know. He may be her husband.*
  It might be cold outside, so I'll take a coat.
- We use ***must*** when we think something is highly probable.
  She's not answering her phone. She must be busy.

Obligation, Prohibition, Necessity, and Advice

- We use ***must*** and ***have to*** to say that it is necessary to do something.
  Visitors must complete the form and then give it to the receptionist.
  We have to fill in this form and then send it to the office.
- We often use ***must*** when the obligation comes from the speaker – it's something the speaker considers important.
  You must do your homework before you go to Greg's house.
  I must get my grandfather a present for his birthday. I forgot last year!
- ***Must*** is followed by an infinitive without *to*.
- We use ***have to*** to say what it is necessary to do.
  You have to answer all the questions on the exam.
  He has to wear a uniform in school.
- We often use ***have to*** when we talk about laws or rules.
  You have to get good exam results to get into this college.
  He's angry because he has to take his hat off in school.
- ***Have to*** is follow by an infinitive without *to*.
- We use ***don't have to*** to say that it is not necessary to do something but that you can do it if you want.
  You don't have to help me with my experiment.
  She doesn't have to get up early tomorrow.
- Question words go at the beginning of the question.
  How much homework do you have to do every day?
  When do we have to make a decision?
- We use ***can't*** and ***must not*** to say something is prohibited by law or rules.
  I can't take my phone to school – it's the rule.
  You must not use your calculator during the exam.
- We use ***need to*** to express necessity in the present. We use ***don't need to*** to show a lack of necessity.
  I need to get home before my parents get angry.
  They don't need to leave now. It's still early.
- We use ***should***(***'nt***) and ***ought to*** to give advice. ***Should***(***'nt***) and ***ought to*** both mean "I (don't) think it's a good idea for someone to do this."
  You should take the bus. It will be faster.
  They shouldn't eat that. They're going to get sick.
  We ought to pay attention. This might be on the exam.

Past Obligation

- We use ***had to*** to say that it was necessary to do something in the past.
  I had to leave school early because I wasn't feeling well.
  They didn't have to come, but they did.
  Did you have to do chores when you were younger?
  Before we took the exam, we had to study a lot.

GRAMMAR PRACTICE

Modals of Deduction and Possibility

1 Circle the correct options.

1. I'm not sure, but I think this gold *may not* / *can't* be real.
2. Reading in bed at night *can* / *must* help you fall asleep faster.
3. I don't know what's in the box. It *could* / *can* be a present.
4. Harry failed two exams. He *couldn't* / *can't* be very happy.
5. Take a drink of water. You *might* / *must* be very thirsty after the game.
6. The doctor's not very sure. She says it *might* / *must* be serious.

2 Use the prompts to write the second sentence.

1. I haven't eaten all day. You / be very hungry
   You must be very hungry.
2. It's eleven o'clock at night. Freya / be in bed
   ____
3. I feel sick. You / need to sit down
   ____
4. That boy looks like Freddie, but Freddie's in Mexico. That / be Freddie
   ____
5. Max got up late. He / not arrive on time for his first class
   ____
6. That cheese is three weeks old! It / be very smelly
   ____

Obligation, Prohibition, Necessity, and Advice

3 Are the sentences about obligation (*O*), prohibition (*P*), necessity (*N*), or advice (*A*)?

1. You must not use your phone in class. P
2. I probably don't need to wear a coat today. ____
3. I think Lauren should study engineering. ____
4. You ought to try turning the computer off. ____
5. You must write at least 100 words. ____
6. What do I have to do to be successful? ____

4 Complete the email with the phrases in the box.

don't have to worry	~~don't need to bring~~
have to take	must not forget
need to pack	ought to buy

Hi Evelyn,

I'm so glad you're coming to visit us. It's really warm here, so you [1] don't need to bring a coat. However, you [2] ________________ your swimsuit because we're going to the beach. We'll [3] ________________ the train, so I [4] ________________ our tickets tomorrow. You [5] ________________ about bringing a towel because we have a lot, but you [6] ________________ your sunscreen!

See you on Friday!

5 Complete the second sentence so that it means the same as the first. Use no more than three words.

1. Don't shout. I can hear everything you're saying.
   You don't need to shout because I can hear everything you say.
2. It's not a very good idea to call him now.
   You probably ________________ him now.
3. I had an appointment with the doctor yesterday.
   I ________________ and see the doctor yesterday.
4. There's no need to worry about making lunch.
   You ________________ to worry about making lunch.
5. No running in the hallways.
   Students ________________ in the hallways.
6. That car must be very expensive.
   That car ________________ cheap.

Past Obligation

6 Complete the sentences about past obligations with the correct form of *have to* and the verb in parentheses.

1. Julieta ________________ (go) to school early on Thursday.
2. Did students ________________ (gather) in the auditorium?
3. She ________________ (not write) another paper.

LANGUAGE BANK

STARTER

Vocabulary

Travel

accommodation backpacking resort
sightseeing tourist attractions trip

Music and Theater

audience lines part
rehearsal scene show

Ways of Communicating

describe greet post shake hands
shout smile translate wave whisper

Grammar in Action

Past and Present, Simple and Continuous
Present Perfect and Simple Past

Writing

Useful Language

Starting and Ending an Informal Email

Hello … / Hi …
How are you? / Thanks for your email. / How are things?
I'm writing to … / I just wanted to say …
See you soon. / Bye for now. / Write back soon.
Take care, … / Love, …

UNIT 1

Vocabulary

Describing Clothes and Shoes

baggy checkered cotton denim
flowery high-heeled leather long-sleeved
plain polka-dot striped tight

Verbs Related to Clothes and Shoes

fit fold go out of style
go with hang up look good on match
unzip wear out zip up

Grammar in Action

Present Perfect Simple and Present Perfect Continuous
Modifiers

Speaking

Everyday English

check out
fashion victim
in
out there

Useful Language

I don't know if …
I'm not a huge fan of …
I think maybe …
That's … uh … different!
They're not exactly my style.

Writing

Useful Language

Great post!
I had no idea that …
It got me thinking about …
Since reading your post, I've …
Thanks for sharing!
We decided to …

LANGUAGE BANK

UNIT 2

Vocabulary

Phrasal Verbs: Changes

do without   end up   go back   go through
look forward to   move out   move to
settle down   sign up   try out
turn down   turn out

Parts of Objects

button   cord   cover   display   handle
key   lens   lid   plug   strap

Grammar in Action

Used To, *Would*, and Simple Past
Past Perfect with *Never*, *Ever*, *Already*, *By* (*Then*), *By the Time*

Speaking

Everyday English

all over again
I'm not surprised.
old-school
That's it.

Useful Language

Is it some kind of …?
I've messed it up.
Like this, you mean?
What you do is, you …
You'll have to …

Writing

Useful Language

first
in addition
in conclusion
second
therefore
this means that

UNIT 3

Vocabulary

Cooking Verbs

bake boil chop fry grate
grill overcook peel roast
season slice spread

Quantities

a bag of a chunk of a cup of a handful of
a piece of a pinch of a slice of
a splash of a spoonful of a sprinkle of

Grammar in Action

Future Forms
Future Continuous and Future Perfect

Speaking

Everyday English

a piece of cake
forever
Is that it?
tasty

Useful Language

Don't forget to … (+ verb)
Once that's done, …
Start by … (+ *-ing*)
While that's … (+ *-ing*)
You'll need …

Writing

Useful Language

… is here to stay
… isn't going anywhere
Watch this space
… will be around forever
… will be the norm

In conclusion, …

LANGUAGE BANK

UNIT 4

Vocabulary

The Five Senses

feel | feel like | look | look like
smell | smell like | sound
sound like | taste | taste like | touch

Describing Texture, Sound, Taste, Etc.

colorful | faint | rough | sharp | shiny
smelly | smooth | sour | spicy | transparent

Grammar in Action

Modals of Deduction and Possibility
Obligation, Prohibition, Necessity, and Advice
Past Obligation

Speaking

Everyday English

Bingo!
I give up!
I guess so.
nice and warm/hot, etc.
Sure, why not?

Useful Language

Guess again.
Guess what it is / they are.
I guess they must be …
Perhaps it's something (+ *adjective*)
They're definitely some kind of …

Writing

Useful Language

According to …
and grew up in …
At the age of …
including …
… is known as …
… was born on …

IRREGULAR VERBS

Infinitive	Simple Past	Past Participle
be	was/were	been
beat	beat	beaten
become	became	become
begin	began	begun
bite	bit	bitten
blow	blew	blown
break	broke	broken
bring	brought	brought
build	built	built
buy	bought	bought
catch	caught	caught
choose	chose	chosen
come	came	come
cost	cost	cost
cut	cut	cut
do	did	done
draw	drew	drawn
drink	drank	drunk
drive	drove	driven
eat	ate	eaten
fall	fell	fallen
feel	felt	felt
fight	fought	fought
find	found	found
fly	flew	flown
forget	forgot	forgotten
get	got	gotten
give	gave	given
go	went	gone
grow	grew	grown
hang	hung	hung
have	had	had
hear	heard	heard
hide	hid	hidden
hit	hit	hit
hold	held	held
hurt	hurt	hurt
keep	kept	kept
know	knew	known
leave	left	left
lend	lent	lent

Infinitive	Simple Past	Past Participle
let	let	let
lie	lied	lied
light	lit	lit
lose	lost	lost
make	made	made
mean	meant	meant
meet	met	met
pay	paid	paid
put	put	put
read	read	read
ride	rode	ridden
ring	rang	rung
rise	rose	risen
run	ran	run
say	said	said
see	saw	seen
sell	sold	sold
send	sent	sent
shine	shone	shone
shoot	shot	shot
show	showed	shown
shut	shut	shut
sing	sang	sung
sit	sat	sat
sleep	slept	slept
speak	spoke	spoken
spend	spent	spent
stand	stood	stood
steal	stole	stolen
swim	swam	swum
take	took	taken
teach	taught	taught
tear	tore	torn
tell	told	told
think	thought	thought
throw	threw	thrown
understand	understood	understood
wake	woke	woken
wear	wore	worn
win	won	won
write	wrote	written

STUDENT'S BOOK ACKNOWLEDGEMENTS

The authors and publishers acknowledge the following sources of copyright material and are grateful for the permissions granted. While every effort has been made, it has not always been possible to identify the sources of all the material used, or to trace all copyright holders. If any omissions are brought to our notice, we will be happy to include the appropriate acknowledgements on reprinting & in the next update to the digital edition, as applicable.

Key: CLIL = Content and Language Integrated Learning; SU = Starter Unit; U = Unit, VB = Vocabulary Bank

Text

U1: Text about Moziah Bridge. Copyrighyt © Adriann Ranta Zurhellen. Reproduced with permission; **U4:** Text about Jordy Cernik. Copyright © Peter Cernik MA aka Jordy. Reproduced with kind permission; Text about Neil Harbisson. Copyright © Neil Harbisson. Reproduced with kind permission; Text about surfer Bethany Hamilton. Copyright © Becky Hamilton. Reproduced with kind permission.

Photography

The following photographs are sourced from Getty Images:

SU: danchooalex/E+; Dave and Les Jacobs/Blend Images; Django/E+; jhorrocks/E+; Vostok/Moment; Lennart Schreiber/EyeEm; Hill Street Studios/Blend Images; yayayoyo/iStock/Getty Images Plus; YasnaTen/iStock/Getty Images Plus; Tigatelu/iStock/Getty Images Plus; Elizabeth Parsons/EyeEm Premium; sbk_20d pictures/Moment; Yavuz Meyveci/iStock Editorial/Getty Images Plus; arabianEye arabianEye; vetdoctor/iStockphoto/Getty Images Plus; **U1:** Westend61; Henrik Sorensen/Stone; Ryan Smith/Corbis; jhorrocks/E+; Halfpoint/iStock/Getty Images Plus; Timur Emek/Getty Images Entertainment; by Lili Ana/Moment Open; Artur Debat/Moment Mobile; Maciej Frolow/The Image Bank; Sidekick/E+; Pascal Deloche/Godong/Corbis Documentary; Chris Ryan/OJO Images; Andy Crawford/Dorling Kindersley; khvost/iStock/Getty Images Plus; GeorgePeters/E+; Paul Simcock; jboater/iStock/Getty Images Plus; Feifei Cui-Paoluzzo/Moment; Leon Bennett/WireImage; mocoo/iStock/Getty Images Plus; ozgurdonmaz/iStock/Getty Images Plus; Jenny Jones/Lonely Planet Images/Getty Images Plus; Erik Isakson; **U2**: Jennifer Perry/EyeEm; mantaphoto/E+; Mark Daffey/Lonely Planet Images; KIKILOMBO/iStock/Getty Images Plus; alejandrophotography/iStock/Getty Images Plus; plherrera/E+; Emanuele Ravecca/EyeEm; Science Photo Library; luoman/E+; Spod/iStock/Getty Images Plus; Steve Shott/Dorling Kindersley; Gregory_DUBUS/iStock/Getty Images Plus; DNY59/E+; Oleg Golovnev/EyeEm; Westend61; Betsie Van der Meer/Stone; ajr_images/iStock/Getty Images Plus; pixdeluxe/iStock/Getty Images Plus; LisaAFischer/iStock/Getty Images Plus; H. Armstrong Roberts/ClassicStock/Archive Photos; Allan Tannenbaum/Archive Photos; Michael Ochs Archives; funky-data/E+; baona/E+; mocoo/iStock/Getty Images Plus; cjmacer/iStock Editorial/Getty Images Plus; **U3**: WIN-Initiative; tgasser/iStock/Getty Images Plus; Jamie Grill/The Image Bank; Andreas Schlegel; Capelle.r/Moment; xujun/Moment; mikroman6/Moment; EasterBunnyUK/iStock/Getty Images Plus; Valentyn Semenov/EyeEm; © 2011 Dorann Weber/Moment Open; Caliphoto/iStock/Getty Images Plus; mikroman6/Moment; Blend Images - JGI/Jamie Grill; Eskay Lim/EyeEm; Jamie Stamey/iStock/Getty Images Plus; Ian Cuming/Ikon Images; NosUA/iStock/Getty Images Plus; D-Keine/E+; Andrey Suslov/iStock/Getty Images Plus; Sirikunkrittaphuk/iStock/Getty Images Plus; Creativ Studio Heinemann; Slawomir Tomas/EyeEm; Maximilian Stock Ltd./Photographer's Choice; Hayley Harrison/The Image Bank; Dorling Kindersley; Pierre-Yves Babelon/Moment; Nickilford/E+; William Whitehurst/Corbis; Klaus Vedfelt/DigitalVision; Maskot; Maica/iStock/Getty Images Plus; Tetra Images; Diana Miller/Cultura; Peter Cade/The Image Bank; marilyna/iStock/Getty Images Plus; Tobias Titz; Hauke Dressler/LOOK-foto/LOOK; Melanitta/iStock/Getty Images Plus; Jami Tarris/Corbis Documentary; GMVozd/E+; Image Source; Rosemary Calvert/Photographer's Choice; Tanya Zouev/StockFood Creative; Neustockimages/iStock/Getty Images Plus; Tim Platt/The Image Bank; Westend61; Rasulovs/iStock/Getty Images Plus; WoodyUpstate/iStock/Getty Images Plus; Joff Lee/Photolibrary; mocoo/iStock/Getty Images Plus; petekarici/E+; Jbryson/iStock/Getty Images Plus; boonsom/iStock/Getty Images Plus; **U4**: Dmytro Ponomarenko/EyeEm; Huntstock; cnicbc/iStock/Getty Images Plus; Tetra Images; Andy Sotiriou/Photodisc; Tai/Moment; Raimund Linke/Oxford Scientific; bugphai/iStock/Getty Images Plus; Jamie Brand/EyeEm; Ian O'Leary/Dorling Kindersley; DragonImages/iStock/Getty Images Plus; bergamont/iStock/Getty Images Plus; Stephen Stickler/Photographer's Choice; Douglas Sacha/Moment; Natthakan Jommanee/EyeEm; Sam Edwards/Sam Edwards; Danita Delimont/Gallo Images; Jutta Klee/Canopy; Jacqui Hurst/Photolibrary; hphimagelibrary/Gallo Images; IAN HOOTON/Science Photo Library; Christian Adams/Photographer's Choice; Coleman515/iStock/Getty Images Plus; kiankhoon/iStock/Getty Images Plus; c11yg/iStock/Getty Images Plus; Buena Vista Images/DigitalVision; AVIcons/iStock/Getty Images Plus; Amin Yusifov/iStock/Getty Images Plus; appleuzr/DigitalVision Vectors; Bruce Mclean/EyeEm; mocoo/iStock/Getty Images Plus; Marko Stavric Photography/Moment/Getty Images Plus; Elena Pueyo/Moment; Arrow/DigitalVision; manoa/Moment; Alberto Ghizzi Panizza/Biosphoto; Davies and Starr/The Image Bank/Getty Images Plus; Mkucova/iStock/Getty Images Plus; **F1**: Anthony Lee/OJO Images; vgajic/E+; Rafael Ben-Ari/The Image Bank; Imgorthand/E+; -VICTOR-/DigitalVision Vectors; **F4**: Nenov/Moment Open; Christopher Daley/500px; MirageC/Moment; PhotoAlto/Odilon Dimier/PhotoAlto Agency RF Collections; **VBS**: Asia-Pacific Images Studio/iStock/Getty Images Plus; Watchara Panyajun/EyeEm; majaiva/E+; Caiaimage/Sam Edwards; LeoPatrizi/E+; Kentaroo Tryman/Maskot; **VB1**: domin_domin/iStock/Getty Images Plus; mawielobob/iStock/Getty Images Plus; Tarzhanova/iStock/Getty Images Plus; kitthanes/iStock/Getty Images Plus; Floortje/E+; Lalouetto/iStock/Getty Images Plus; Mehmet Hilmi Barcin/E+; FlamingPumpkin/iStock/Getty Images Plus; Rermrat Kaewpukdee/EyeEm; Ng Sok Lian/EyeEm; **VB2**: Karl Tapales/Moment; JuergenBosse/iStock/Getty Images Plus; Melanie Hobson/EyeEm; kk2s/iStock/Getty Images Plus; MartinPrescott/E+; Gado Images/Photodisc; TARIK KIZILKAYA/E+; Jorge Alberto Bohorquez Suarez/EyeEm; LeMusique/iStock/Getty Images Plus; Somsak Bumroongwong/EyeEm; **VB3**: tirc83/iStock/Getty Images Plus; Westend61; UpperCut Images; Paula ./FOAP; KucherAV/iStock/Getty Images Plus; dlewis33/E+; Lucy Lambriex/DigitalVision; Adam Radosavljevic/EyeEm; lolostock/iStock/Getty Images Plus; uuurska/iStock/Getty Images Plus; Lakshmi3/iStock/Getty Images Plus; Capelle.r/Moment; **VB4**: Dalia Rady/EyeEm; Imagevixen/RooM; DragonFly/iStock/Getty Images Plus; Pierre-Yves Babelon/Antananarivo, Antananarivo Province, Madagascar; Mike Whitby/EyeEm; malerapaso/E+; stockstudioX/E+; Stefka Pavlova/Moment; Theerapan Bhumirat/EyeEm; luknaja/iStock/Getty Images Plus; **CLIL2**: Bettmann; Thinkstock Images/Stockbyte; **CLIL4**: VICTOR HABBICK VISIONS/SCIENCE PHOTO LIBRARY.

The following photographs are sourced from other libraries/sources:

U1—U4: Carboxylase/Shutterstock; **U4**: Copyright © Peter Cernik MA aka Jordy; Copyright © Neil Harbisson.

Illustrations

SU: Sean Longcroft; **U2,** Claire Rollet (Illustration Web); **U2, U4:** Joanna Kerr.

Video Stills

The following stills are sourced from Getty Images:

US: Feng Wei Photography/Moment; **U1**: Alexander Spatari/Moment; FG Trade/Creatas Video; Merlas/iStock/Getty Images Plus; **U2**: RWP UK/DigitalVision; Sirinarth Mekvorawuth/EyeEm; Getty Images/EyeEm; taavet/Creatas Video+; **U3**: Neustockimages/Creatas Video+; Besjunior/iStock/Getty Images Plus; andresr/Creatas Video; **U4**: nattanan726/Creatas Video+; gpointstudio/Creatas Video+/Getty Images Plus; yacobchuk/iStock/Getty Images Plus.

Cover Design and Illustrations: Collaborate Agency

Video Production: Lucentum Digital

Audio Recordings: Eastern Sky Studios

Typesetting: Aphik, S.A. de C.V.

Contributing authors: Daniel Vincent, Liz Walter, and Kate Woodford

Versioner: Suzanne Harris

American English Consultant: Multimodal Media

Freelance Editors: Mandie Drucker, Penny Nicholson, Cara Norris-Ramirez, and Rebecca Raynes

The authors and editors would like to thank all the teachers and consultants who have contributed to the development of the course, in particular:

Mexico: Ana Belem Duran; Nelly Marina Elizalde; Julio Andrés Franco Del Campo; Nimbe García Haro; Raoul Josset Paquette; Adriana Maldonado Torres; Ana Edith Ramos Ramírez

Brazil: Beatriz Affonso; Alessandra Bautista; Ana Carolina De Luca; Esdras Fattobene; Maria Claudia Ferreira; Itana Lins; Maria Helena Meyer; Valéria Moraes Novoa; Odinéia Morandi; Regina Pedroso De Araujo; Andrea Perina; Simone Rodrigues; Jacqueline Saback; Clice Sales; Silvia Teles

Turkey: Belgün Akçelik; Peggy Alptekin; Hayri Arslan; Ayşe Aylin Kündüroğlu; Nihan Çalışkan; Selin Dinçkal Erkenci; Bengü Özbek; Saliha Şimşek

WORKBOOK ACKNOWLEDGEMENTS

The authors and publishers acknowledge the following sources of copyright material and are grateful for the permissions granted. While every effort has been made, it has not always been possible to identify the sources of all the material used, or to trace all copyright holders. If any omissions are brought to our notice, we will be happy to include the appropriate acknowledgements on reprinting & in the next update to the digital edition, as applicable.

Key: SU = Starter Unit, U = Unit.

Photography

The following photographs are sourced from Getty Images:

SU: Harald Nachtmann/Moment; Anestis Karagiannopoulos/EyeEm; Matteo Colombo/DigitalVision; oleksii arseniuk/iStock/Getty Images Plus; Anastasiia_M/iStock/Getty Images Plus; chokkicx/DigitalVision Vectors; primeimages/iStock/Getty Images Plus; Nikada/iStock/Getty Images Plus; JohnnyGreig/E+; platongkoh/iStock/Getty Images Plus; Hans Neleman/Stone; Hemera Technologies/PhotoObjects.net; SDI Productions/E+; John Cancalosi/Photolibrary; Hill Street Studios/DigitalVision; **U1**: ArnaPhoto/iStock/Getty Images Plus; Sadeugra/E+; ferrantraite/iStock/Getty Images Plus; JackF/iStock/Getty Images Plus; Chiyacat/iStock/Getty Images Plus; rolfbodmer/E+; Jitalia17/E+; skodonnell/E+; CSA Images/Vetta; **U2**: Julie Moquet/EyeEm; Ariel Skelley/DigitalVision; JRL/The Image Bank/Getty Images Plus; Don Mason; Getty Images/Aurora Creative; Image Source; Ljupco/iStock/Getty Images Plus; slobo/iStock/Getty Images Plus; hh5800/iStock/Getty Images Plus; homydesign/iStock/Getty Images Plus; Bet_Noire/iStock/Getty Images Plus; Valerie Loiseleux/iStock/Getty Images Plus; Whiteway/iStock/Getty Images Plus; Getty Images/Caiaimage; Debrocke/ClassicStock/Archive Photos; kertlis/E+; PM Images/DigitalVision; Wan Muhammad Faisalludin Wan Azeland/EyeEm; Peter Dazeley/The Image Bank; Richard Newstead/Moment; Oliver Cleve/Photographer's Choice; TommL/E+; Nicholas Eveleigh/Photodisc; ET-ARTWORKS/DigitalVision Vectors; NiseriN/iStock/Getty Images Plus; **U3**: Getty Images/Dorling Kindersley; Guillermo Murcia/Moment Open; Jody Louie took this picture/Moment; Joy Skipper/Photolibrary; Giles Clarke/Getty Images News; Gavin Hellier/robertharding/Getty Images Plus; Rosemary Calvert/The Image Bank Unreleased; alantobey/E+; Anne Ackermann/DigitalVision; George Mdivanian/EyeEm; erierika/iStock/Getty Images Plus; Getty Images/StockFood; Simon McGill/Moment; Chris Everard/The Image Bank/Getty Images Plus; anna1311/iStock/Getty Images Plus; Christian Vierig/Getty Images Entertainment; Evgeniyaphotography/iStock/Getty Images Plus; -slav-/iStock/Getty Images Plus; imaginima/iStock/Getty Images Plus; H. Armstrong Roberts/ClassicStock/Archive Photos; Highwaystarz-Photography/iStock/Getty Images Plus; **U4**: Elizaveta Pahomova/EyeEm; kiszon pascal/Moment; Guillaume CHANSON/Moment; Kristina Strasunske/Moment; Getty Images/Caiaimage; Johann van Heerden/Moment Open; Nenov/Moment Open; briddy_/iStock/Getty Images Plus; Ed Freeman/Stone; Sally Anscombe/DigitalVision; Henrik Sorensen/DigitalVision; Glynne Joseph Pritchard/Moment Mobile; Noam Galai/Getty Images Entertainment; Toni Anne Barson/FilmMagic; Fuse/Corbis.

Illustrations

U1: Claire Rollet; **U3:** Joanna Kerr; **U4:** Howarth from The Big Red illustration.

Cover Design and Illustrations: Collaborate Agency

Audio Recordings: Eastern Sky Studios

Typesetting: Aphik, S.A. de C.V.

American English Consultant: Mandie Drucker

Freelance Editors: Sue Costello, Jacqueline French, Bastian Harris, and Penny Nicholson